T0325327

Founded in 1972, the Institute for Research on Public Policy is an independent, national, nonprofit organization. Its mission is to improve public policy in Canada by promoting and contributing to a policy process that is more broadly based, informed and effective.

In pursuit of this mission, the IRPP

- identifies significant public policy questions that will confront Canada in the longer term future and undertakes independent research into these questions;

- promotes wide dissemination of key results from its own and other research activities;

- encourages non-partisan discussion and criticism of public policy issues in a manner which elicits broad participation from all sectors and regions of Canadian society and links research with processes of social learning and policy formation.

The IRPP's independence is assured by an endowment fund, to which federal and provincial governments and the private sector have contributed.

Créé en 1972, l'Institut de recherche en politiques publiques est un organisme national et indépendant à but non lucratif.

L'IRPP a pour mission de favoriser le développement de la pensée politique au Canada par son appui et son apport à un processus élargi, plus éclairé et plus efficace d'élaboration et d'expression des politiques publiques.

Dans le cadre de cette mission, l'IRPP a pour mandat :

- d'identifier les questions politiques auxquelles le Canada sera confronté dans l'avenir et d'entreprendre des recherches indépendantes à leur sujet;

- de favoriser une large diffusion des résultats les plus importants de ses propres recherches et de celles des autres sur ces questions;

- de promouvoir une analyse et une discussion objectives des questions politiques de manière à faire participer activement au débat public tous les secteurs de la société canadienne et toutes les régions du pays, et à rattacher la recherche à l'évolution sociale et à l'élaboration de politiques.

L'indépendance de l'IRPP est assurée par les revenus d'un fonds de dotation auquel ont souscrit les gouvernements fédéral et provinciaux, ainsi que le secteur privé.

INSTITUTE FOR RESEARCH ON PUBLIC POLICY

INSTITUT DE RECHERCHE EN POLITIQUES PUBLIQUES

canada:

RECLAIMING THE MIDDLE GROUND

DONALD G. LENIHAN
GORDON ROBERTSON
ROGER TASSÉ

IRPP
GOVERNANCE

Printed in Canada

Bibliothèque nationale du Québec
Dépôt légal 1994

Canadian Cataloguing in Publication Data

Lenihan, Donald G.
Canada : reclaiming the middle ground

Includes bibliographical references.

ISBN 0-88645-167-1

1. Federal government—Canada.   2. Canada—Politics and government.
I. Robertson, Gordon, 1917- . II. Tassé, Roger, 1931- .
III. Institute for Research on Public Policy. IV. Title.

JL65 1994.L45 1994   320.471'049   C94-900862-1

Marye Bos
Director of Publications, IRPP

F. Leslie Seidle
Research Director, Governance Program, IRPP

Copy Editor
Mathew Horsman

Design and Production
Ric Little and Barbara Rosenstein

Cover Illustration
Barbara Rosenstein

Published by
The Institute for Research on Public Policy (IRPP)
L'Institut de recherche en politiques publiques
1470 Peel Street, Suite 200
Montreal, Quebec H3A 1T1

Distributed by
Renouf Publishing Co. Ltd.
1294 Algoma Road
Ottawa, Ontario K1B 3W8
For orders, call 613-741-4333
or fax 613-741-5439

TABLE OF CONTENTS

FOREWORD

Analysts and commentators have often claimed that the middle ground in Canadian politics is crowded territory. Their argument is that, in a country marked by diversity – whether regional, linguistic, socio-demographic or other – public policy has to be based on compromise. They labelled the process for arriving at such agreement "brokerage politics." In addition, so went the argument, political parties, at least those with the ambition of forming a government, responded to a so-called reality of electoral dynamics: when the voters in the middle of the spectrum are much more numerous than those with more extreme views, leaders need to modulate their stance and avoid the hard edges of major issues.

A number of developments, including the results of the 1993 federal election, have called into question this conception of the Canadian political process. The authors of this book examine some of the symptoms of the shift, notably the polarization of positions and discourse during the past decade or so on a number of fundamental issues related to the structure of the Canadian federation and our political culture: the distinctiveness and aspirations of Quebec; regional (especially Western) "alienation"; Aboriginal self-government; and the impact of the Canadian Charter of Rights and Freedoms. While this polarization may have been particularly evident during the Meech Lake and Charlottetown constitutional rounds, the authors' exploration extends well beyond this realm as they seek to explain why so many have vacated the middle ground.

In their conclusion, the authors indicate that this book "was written in the conviction that the federal system, with its basic acceptance of diversity and its capacity to adapt and change, has been essential to the success of Canada as a country, and that reclaiming these two virtues – respect for diversity and flexibility – is vital for its future." More specifically, they contend that the present constitutional framework allows considerable room to accommodate moderate Quebec nationalism, Aboriginal peoples' desire to govern themselves, regional differences and the need to balance individual rights with the interests of communities. In the authors' view, some constitutional amendments may eventually prove necessary (these are summarized in the conclusion), but they would be few in number and each would be considered on its merits rather than as part of what Peter Russell calls "mega constitutional politics." In the meantime, they argue, the *status quo* is not an option: change is inevitable as globalization proceeds, the interdependence of governments in Canada becomes even more marked and citizens and groups pursue (including through the courts) new avenues for integrating freedom and equality with diversity.

Canada: Reclaiming the Middle Ground is being published as part of IRPP's Governance project, "Canadian Federalism: Options for Change," which is intended to address the fundamental issue of Quebec's place within Canada and other questions about how to structure and govern a country of diverse communities and multiple identities. The release of this book follows publication of *Seeking a New Canadian Partnership: Asymmetrical and Confederal Options,* the proceedings of a national conference IRPP held in Toronto on June 22, 1994.

The authors of the present volume, whose rich experience informs their work, call for Canadians to reform the way they think and talk about Canada – in particular, to see federalism "more as a process than a structure." Their reasoned and reasonable discussion provides a strong case for doing so. While the views expressed here are those of the authors and do not necessarily reflect the opinion of IRPP or its Board of Directors, we are pleased to be associated with this project. We hope that reading the pages that follow will lead many Canadians to reflect on the basis and future of our federal union, and that they will share their ideas with others as part of an enriched public debate.

Monique Jérôme-Forget
President, IRPP

INTRODUCTION

The clearest lesson of the debate over the 1992 Charlottetown Accord is that Canadians are divided in their vision of the country. Yet we are convinced that a relatively coherent vision is essential to good government – particularly in an era of intense restructuring. How is this dilemma to be solved?

In this book, we wrestle with that question. The project began in the wake of the referendum on the Charlottetown Accord. The time seemed right to reflect on some of the deep differences over politics and country that surfaced during the debate. The question we asked ourselves was whether the basis for a workable federal arrangement still exists. Now, a year and a half later, with the *Bloc québécois* forming the Official Opposition in Ottawa, the Reform party a close second, the *Parti québécois* in power in Quebec and a referendum on the horizon, the question seems as pertinent as ever. Our answer is that federalism remains not only a viable, but the best, option.

Our study examines how the political philosophy of liberalism – especially as incorporated into "pan-Canadianism" under former Prime Minister Pierre Trudeau – contrasts and conflicts with the more federalist aspirations of moderate Quebec nationalists, western regionalists and Aboriginal peoples. We then work toward a synthesis.

Here "globalization" lends a hand. Global trends are putting both liberalism and federalism into a new perspective. In western democracies, traditional views on the state, sovereignty and the nature of citizenship are being reformulated, in response to increasing economic integration, the communications revolution and the growing importance of international and regional trade arrangements. As a result, we argue, the two Canadian traditions of liberalism and federalism are starting to look complementary, rather than antagonistic.

However, after 25 years of constitutional negotiations, Canadians are tired of such debates. As a result, they have become distrustful of, and often irritated by, complex, sometimes ambiguous, accounts of federalism. The temptation is strong to side with those who cast the issues in stark and often categorical terms: "Federalism is inherently centralizing!" or "All provinces are equal!" or "No special rights!" Claims such as these do crystallize the options. But they also misrepresent reality.

Treating rules of thumb as absolute principles removes the middle ground from the debate, thus polarizing opinion. Hence, on the Quebec question, many now see only two choices: the *status quo* or independence. This underestimates both the flexibility of federalism and the need for accommodation if Canada is to survive. It also suggests that meaningful reform must begin with constitutional amendment. But the system is not that rigid. If it were, it would fail not only Quebecers, but also First Nations and those with a more regional vision of Canada.

The temptation to use slogans like axioms must be resisted. Allowing our federalist discourse to be overrun by categorical language would be a calamity. Canadian federalism is, first and foremost, about preserving the middle ground. That requires flexibility, nuance and a spirit of accommodation.

This book explores the middle ground. It examines some of the ambiguous language and complex concepts that underlie Canadian federalism. While we consider the constitutional debates of the last 30 years, the book is not about the Constitution as such; nor is it a chronicle of Canadians' long constitutional odyssey or an analysis of the politics around it. It is a reflection on Canadian political culture.

Our goal is to provoke Canadians to think and talk about how they think and talk about Canadian federalism. How they think and talk about it is crucial to how they practice it. And, in our view, the *practice* of federalism urgently needs reform. As history has shown, much can be done without changing a word in the Constitution. Thus, even if we agree that constitutional reform is desirable but unlikely in the immediate future, we do not think it follows that, for federalists, the *status quo* is the only or the best option.

Indeed, the *status quo* is not really an option at all. Taken together, the national unity question, globalization and high public debt mean that major change is all but certain. Self-government arrangements are being negotiated with Aboriginal peoples. Federal and provincial governments have committed themselves to a new interprovincial trade agreement. Serious efforts are under way to streamline the federal system by eliminating overlap and duplication. And an overhaul of income security and labour adjustment programs is on the agenda.

Add to this the North American Free Trade Agreement and the new trade deal under the General Agreement on Tariffs and Trade and it becomes clear that the real question is not whether Canadians should accept the *status quo* – that is already gone – but whether they have a collective vision for the future, one that will help them shape and adjust to what is in effect a new environment. It is on this level that we hope the present book makes a contribution.

We outline here a vision for Canada, one we hope most Canadians may find acceptable. Real change in the way federalism operates will require the enunciation of shared goals and principles; determining answers to questions that arise from the *practice* of federalism requires first that we chart the middle ground of Canadian political culture.

The volume is divided into three parts. Part 1 explores the Canadian commitment to federalism and the tensions that have arisen between federalism and liberalism, especially as a result of adoption in 1982 of the Canadian Charter of Rights and Freedoms.

Part 2 sketches an approach to Canadian federalism that aims at accommodating diversity without undermining either individual freedom and equality or the sense of shared community. The essence of our own position is found in these chapters.

Part 3 is the most practical of the three. It works out some of the implications of our approach for the three main problem areas identified in Part 1: Aboriginal self-government, western regionalism and the question of Quebec's place in Confederation.

ACKNOWLEDGEMENTS

This book has taken far longer than any of us expected. It is the product of many meetings, discussions and drafts. Many people helped along the way with comments. We would especially like to thank Gérald Beaudoin, André Burelle, Alan Cairns, Théo Geraets, Rob Howse, Monique Jérôme-Forget, Will Kymlicka, Guy Laforest, Peter Russell, Ron Stevenson and the anonymous reviewer for the Institute for Research on Public Policy, all of whom read and helpfully commented on various parts of the text at some point in its evolution. Our special thanks to Leslie Seidle, Research Director of IRPP's Governance Program, for his dedication and helpful comments in preparing the manuscript for publication; and to Mathew Horsman for his efficient work in copy-editing the text.

Thanks are also due to our colleagues at the Network on the Constitution who lent their support. Finally, we would like to express our appreciation to the federal Department of Justice for a contribution that helped finance the project.

LIBERALISM, FEDERALISM AND CANADIAN POLITICAL CULTURE

1

ARE CANADIANS
CAUGHT IN A POLITICAL
CATCH-22?

"ABSTRACT" VS. "ISSUE-BY-ISSUE" APPROACH

The intensity of the reaction in Quebec following the collapse of the Meech Lake Accord in 1990 stunned many in English-speaking Canada. The surge in support for sovereignty that followed sent shudders through the political class in the rest of Canada. By way of contrast, October 27, 1992, the day after the referendum on the Charlottetown Accord, was relatively quiet and unemotional. The fact that the Accord was spurned in so many quarters seems to have carried the merciful consequence that no region or group could claim to have been isolated or rejected by the rest. The stunning swiftness with which the country then turned its attention to other matters only underlined the extent to which, after several years of intense constitutional discussion, Canadians had simply had enough. Clearly, they wanted governments to forget the Constitution and focus attention on finding solutions to the more practical and immediate problems of slow economic growth and high unemployment.

Since then, this theme has often been sounded by academics, pundits and policy analysts who insist that, in the post-Charlottetown era, governments should focus on practical problems, in specific policy areas, approach them one at a time and deal with each on its own merits. They should avoid trying to solve issues and problems at too abstract a level. We can call this the "issue-by-issue approach."

Insofar as the issue-by-issue approach helps steer governments away from the constitutional quagmire, it is not only a wise but an unimpeachable strategy. If a

1

single lesson can be gleaned from the Canada Round, it seems to be that the constitutional debate has become caught up in abstractions and conflicts over symbolism that, as things stand, lead nowhere. Nevertheless, putting the issue-by-issue approach into practice is more difficult than many of its advocates seem to realize. For, impressions notwithstanding, the difference between the "issue-by-issue approach" and the "abstract" one of the constitutional rounds is really one of degree rather than of kind. There is no way to address the "issues" without taking a position on abstract values such as equality and diversity, if only implicitly. Perhaps the best way to make this point is through an example.

At a series of workshops on federalism[1] a participant argued that the language of the social policy debate in Canada was mired in "myths," many of which could be traced back to the constitutional debates. He cited the use of the language of "national standards." Insofar as there are government-imposed requirements on, say, health care, he noted, they are far more general than most people think. They do not, for example, cover levels of service or content. They are confined to very general conditions such as accessibility, portability and the like.[2] Yet the public debate over health care focuses on whether Canadians' commitment to equality implies a commitment to maintaining "national standards." The result, continued the participant, is a sterile debate over the meaning of abstract concepts such as "equality" and "diversity" – a debate that is simply detached from real policy issues.

As things stand, concluded the participant, there are two relatively unconnected discourses in which social policy is debated. One takes place in newspapers and over the air-waves. It is usually based upon "myths" and justified in terms of empty abstractions. The other typically occurs among policy analysts. Its key terms and arguments are based upon detailed and often highly technical analyses of the issues and problems that define some policy field.

The participant's comments help explain the sense of alienation felt by the general public from the political class: on public policy issues, the two groups not only "speak different languages," they are concerned with different things. The analysis suggests that the way to close the gap is to purge public debate of some of the "myths" that inform it. In particular, we should shun the kind of abstract discussions about identity, equality and diversity that were encouraged during the constitutional rounds. Still, as it stands, this is itself a pretty "abstract" piece of advice. What does it mean in concrete terms?

This, presumably, is where the injunction to proceed issue-by-issue is supposed to help. The "issue-by-issue" approach suggests that (a) there are already a number of important issues that demand attention; and (b) the way to make progress on them is to analyze each on its own merits with a view to arriving at a reasonable solution. But consider the following list of federal-provincial issues. The federal government:

(1) should (not) use its "trade and commerce" or "peace, order and good government" powers in the Constitution to strike down interprovincial trade barriers;

(2) should (not) give up its control over labour market training;

(3) should (not) provide regionally differentiated unemployment insurance (UI) benefits;

(4) should (not) concern itself with regional economic development;

(5) should (not) give the provinces a greater role in negotiating international trade agreements;

(6) should (not) remove itself from health care;

(7) should (not) get involved in education;

(8) should (not) attach performance requirements to transfer payments for health or education;

(9) should (not) give the provinces more control over immigration.

To say that each of these issues can be discussed "on its own merits" is more than a bit misleading. The fact is, the issues in policy areas such as immigration, education, social assistance, UI, health care and labour market training cannot be isolated. Increasing the number of immigrants, for example, will have consequences in all the other areas. This sort of interdependence is now widely recognized.[3]

The injunction to take issues one at a time and "on their own merits" therefore must be taken with a large grain of salt. A government that takes it too literally risks ending up with a series of policy conflicts. It will not do to say that conflicts can be avoided by respecting "rational criteria" such as efficiency and accountability. At the end of the day, a coherent policy agenda will require choices from among a number of broad, sometimes competing, objectives that the federal government may wish to promote, such as regional equity, equality of opportunity, respect for diversity, provincial autonomy, linguistic duality, international competitiveness or a sense of national identity.

Taking the issue-by-issue approach at face value suggests that "real" disagreements over policy are by and large over how best to solve specific issues and technical problems in a given policy area. This suggests that the solution is better technical information. Without underestimating the importance of such information, we underline that, in fact, what often makes a federal-provincial issue an *issue* is not a disagreement that will be solved in this way. It is a clash over the *values* perceived to be at stake.

Consider, for example, (1) from the list above. The question of the extent of the federal government's role in strengthening the economic union – indeed, even the question of what, precisely, this union entails – is deeply philosophical in that it cannot be thoroughly analyzed without considering a host of very basic questions about individual freedom, social justice and the nature of provincial autonomy.[4]

In short, even if it is accepted that the issue-by-issue injunction is a good one – and there is no attempt to deny it here – good government requires what we will call a *vision* of the political community: a set of over-arching values and objectives that policy aims at promoting. But getting Canadians to endorse such a vision *necessarily involves them in reflection and debate about their commitments to fundamental values such as freedom, equality and diversity.* We agree with the participant at the workshop: there is a danger in overemphasizing a "top down" approach to politics. But we reply that there are also dangers in overemphasizing a "bottom up" approach. In practice, public debate and reflection should interact with, inform and transform one another.[5]

Two lessons can be drawn. First, trying to purge Canadians' public policy debates of high-level normative concepts such as equality, freedom and diversity is really an ostrich-like attempt to avoid coming to terms with some of their most serious and substantial disagreements. Second, the best strategy for reforming or "demythologizing" their political discourse – the one we pursue here – is to strive for a greater measure of consensus on how such terms are to be understood in Canadian political debate.

The Political Catch-22

If, as we claim, good government requires a vision, and if Canadians have arrived at irreconcilable visions of their country, a menacing conclusion looms. Canadians may have developed a political culture with a built-in catch-22: they cannot govern effectively without uniting citizens around a relatively coherent vision of the country;

but trying to rally them around such a vision only further divides them. It is therefore fair to ask whether a national leader who, acting on our advice, develops, implements and defends a policy agenda based on a particular vision of the country is likely only to plunge Canadians into another national unity debate. Is it possible to develop a vision that does not run up against the catch-22? And if so, how?

Since the contemporary constitutional odyssey began in 1968 under Prime Minister Pearson, the federal approach to federalism has been dominated by two broad themes: national unity and managing the federation. The former was defined largely in response to the constitutional objectives of successive Quebec governments – although by the mid-1970s, most other provincial governments had begun to advance their own objectives. The second theme was an attempt to strengthen the country by developing policies based on the political, social and economic philosophy of the post-Second World War welfare state.

These two themes merged in the Trudeau government's attempt to develop and project a pan-Canadian vision of the political community. Such a vision, it was hoped, would help Canadians transcend the deepening regional and other cleavages within the country. The effort culminated in the Constitution Act, 1982 which included a Charter of Rights, entrenchment of certain principles of the Official Languages Act, recognition of Aboriginal rights, a clearer definition of provincial powers over natural resources and a constitutional commitment to equalization.[6] All were central to what had come to be seen as a project in *nation building*. Unfortunately, the agreement reached in 1981 was not endorsed by the Quebec government; nor has any Quebec government since endorsed it, despite great efforts.

Our point of departure in this book is the belief that the pan-Canadian vision behind the nation-building approach to federalism of recent years must be modified. There are at least three reasons:

- the twin failures of the Meech Lake and Charlottetown accords seem to have brought to a head a deep "philosophical difference" within Canadian society over certain aspects of pan-Canadianism; as a result, mega constitutional politics[7] has been discredited as a possible solution to the country's unresolved regional, linguistic and cultural, tensions – at least for the foreseeable future;
- the current fiscal crisis has undermined the federal government's ability to maintain, let alone expand, the web of programs developed in the 1960s and 1970s,

and has produced a new range of problems for which the Constitution may not be directly relevant;

- "globalization" appears to be altering the economic and social basis of the federation in ways that could fundamentally change the nature of federal-provincial relations over the next decade.

The task of this book is to reflect on what sort of vision might complete or replace the pan-Canadian one. We do not agree, however, with those who think that the house must be razed to its foundations. There is much we accept in the pan-Canadian vision. We assume as well that constitutional reform is not the only place to begin. A full response to some longstanding issues in the national unity debate may require changes to the Constitution; but we are not convinced that reform must – or even *should* – begin there. Real progress at the constitutional level will require greater consensus among Canadians on how to think and talk about the country. The focus here is thus on political culture rather than constitutional reform.[8]

We think the ongoing national unity debate is in large part a result of Canadians' failure to come to terms with two conflicting but equally legitimate ways that they think and talk about their political community. On the one hand, there is a rich federalist tradition in Canadian politics that emphasizes a commitment to respect the country's regional, linguistic and cultural diversity. On the other hand, Canadians are deeply committed to the political and moral tradition of liberal democracy, with its emphasis on individual freedom and equality.

Canadians have failed to unite the two traditions of liberalism and federalism within a single, relatively coherent vision of their country. Instead, a number of conflicting visions have emerged, some emphasizing the commitment to diversity, some to freedom, some to equality. This has destabilized the political culture. If the country is to avoid the political catch-22 and find a vision around which it can unite, Canadians need to integrate better these different – often conflicting – viewpoints and the political discourses to which they give rise.

The first step is to distinguish between a political vision in the usual sense – i.e., a set of objectives that policy aims to promote – and a more comprehensive kind of political vision, what we call a *meta-vision* for Canada. By this we mean more than a political vision in the usual sense. We have in mind something more comprehensive: a meta-vision defines the "ground rules" for a polity. It is a set of over-arching principles, values or commitments in terms of which the legitimacy of competing visions, and of the decision-making process itself, can be debated and evaluated.[9]

Canadians presently lack a set of common ground rules. A realignment of their underlying commitments to liberalism and federalism may provide this. Our effort to achieve such a realignment leads to a kind of pluralism that goes beyond liberalism without abandoning it. We call this *federal pluralism*. The following chapters explore that concept and suggest how it might help stabilize Canadian political culture. Our reflections are thus motivated by the conviction that traditional liberal philosophy fails to address all the needs of a large, multinational and polyethnic, post-industrial, liberal-democratic federation such as Canada.

Notes

1. The series was organized by the Network on the Constitution during July and August 1993 around the theme "New Forces and Canadian Federalism."

2. See Peter M. Leslie, "The Fiscal Crisis of Canadian Federalism," in *A Partnership in Trouble: Renegotiating Fiscal Federalism* (Toronto: C.D. Howe Institute, 1993), pp. 29-30.

3. See Peter Leslie, *Federal State, National Economy* (Toronto: University of Toronto Press, 1987), chap. 4.

4. See Robert Howse, *Economic Union, Social Justice, and Constitutional Reform: Towards A High But Level Playing Field* (Toronto: York University Centre for Public Law and Public Policy, 1992), pp. 1-17.

5. The approach is similar to what John Rawls famously called the method of "reflective equilibrium." See John Rawls, *A Theory of Justice* (Cambridge: Harvard University Press, 1979), pp. 48-51.

6. Equalization is a system for redistributing wealth from the richer to the less well-off provinces. The federal government raises the money through taxes and then redistributes it to the provinces on the basis of a complicated formula. The principle was entrenched at the time of patriation in section 36 of the Constitution Act, 1982.

7. The term "mega constitutional politics" was coined by Peter Russell in his very readable book *Constitutional Odyssey: Can Canadians Be A Sovereign People?* (Toronto: University of Toronto Press, 1992), p. 75. He writes:

> Constitutional politics at the mega level is distinguished in two ways from normal constitutional politics. First, mega constitutional politics goes beyond disputing the merits of specific constitutional proposals and addresses the very nature of the political community on which the constitution is based. Mega constitutional politics, whether directed towards comprehensive constitutional change or not, is concerned with reaching agreement on the identity and fundamental principles of the body politic. The second feature of mega constitutional politics flows logically from the first. Precisely because of the fundamental nature of the issues in dispute – their tendency to touch citizens' sense of identity and self-worth – mega constitutional politics is exceptionally emotional and intense. When a country's constitutional politics reaches this level, the constitutional question tends to dwarf all other public concerns.

8. By "political culture" we mean, broadly, the politically relevant attitudes, values, beliefs and practices of a group of people. For a discussion of the history and evolution of the concept of political culture, see David V.J. Bell, *The Roots of Disunity: A Study of Canadian Political Culture*, revised ed. (Toronto: Oxford University Press, 1992), chap. 1.

9. In a manuscript entitled *Le mal canadien*, planned for publication in 1995, André Burelle develops a parallel concept which he refers to as a "meta-culture."

2

LIBERALISM AND FEDERALISM: SURVEYING THE TERRAIN

WHY IS CANADA A FEDERATION?

Canada is – and always has been – regionally, socially and culturally diverse. In 1867, the Founding Fathers faced the task of building a country out of a handful of colonies with too much geography, too few people, and two different linguistic and cultural groups. The leaders of the Canadas, Nova Scotia and New Brunswick saw important advantages in a union of the colonies, but they were conscious – or became conscious – of the need to accept something less than full unity, if it was to be achieved at all. George Brown put it clearly in the debate in the Legislative Assembly of Canada in 1865:

> Here is a people composed of two distinct races, speaking different languages, with religious and social and municipal and educational institutions totally different; with sectional hostilities of such a character as to render government for many years well-nigh impossible; with a Constitution so unjust in the view of one section as to justify any resort to enforce a remedy.[1]

And after going into the facts of geography and distance, Brown continued about the choice of federalism:

> But there is another reason why the union was not made legislative – it could not be carried. We had either to take a Federal union or drop the negotiation. Not only were our friends from Lower Canada against it, but so were most of

the delegates from the Maritime Provinces. There was but one choice open to us – Federal union or nothing.[2]

John A. Macdonald was equally clear about the necessity of federalism or no union at all:

> ...I have never hesitated to state my own opinions. I have again and again stated in the House, that, if practicable, I thought a Legislative union would be preferable...But, on looking at the subject in the Conference, and discussing the matter as we did, most unreservedly, and with a desire to arrive at a satisfactory conclusion, we found that such a system was impracticable.[3]

Thus, federalism was as a way of achieving union while accommodating what the Fathers saw as the two most important forms of diversity in the proposed new country: the regional distinctions between the Maritime provinces (Nova Scotia and New Brunswick) and Upper and Lower Canada; and the linguistic and cultural distinctions between French- and English-speaking Canadians.

But if it is true that the Fathers recognized the need to accommodate diversity through federalism, it is also true that when the British North America Act was drawn up some of its authors viewed the new state as close to a unitary one. The inclusion of certain measures suggested to them that the central government would play the dominant role.[4] The presence of these "centralizing elements" in the Act has even resulted in later commentators referring to the original union as quasi-federal.[5] In the first century after Confederation, however, judicial interpretation leaned toward a stronger role for the provinces.[6] This, in turn, encouraged the development of a strong federalist political culture within the new country. As a result, the idea of federalism as a means of accommodating diversity has strengthened over the years.

With Canada now covering most of the northern half of the continent, the emergence of the global economy and the new awareness of the need to fit Aboriginal peoples into our constitutional structure, the concerns over diversity remain as central to Canadian politics as in 1867. Consistent with this, we view the choice of federalism as a general commitment that *the federal task of promoting Canadians' common interests will be subject to, or restrained by, a general respect for the regional, cultural and linguistic diversity of the country.*[7]

CANADIAN FEDERALISM: OF VISIONS AND META-VISIONS

Canada, however, is not just a federal state. It is also a liberal-democratic one. As such, it is a hybrid. Liberal democracy and federalism belong to separate (though overlapping) traditions. Many liberal democracies, such as France, are not federal states and some federal states, such as the former Soviet Union, are not liberal democracies. In a number of countries, the two traditions have been united to produce remarkably stable polities with a high quality of life. Examples include Australia, Switzerland, the United States (after the Civil War) and the Federal Republic of Germany. The success of these countries suggests that the two traditions are not inherently incompatible. On the contrary, they seem in many ways complementary.

As the debates of the last 30 years attest, Canadians have been far less successful at integrating the two traditions in a single, stable political culture. Indeed, their juxtaposition has encouraged the development of two divergent, and often conflicting, visions of the Canadian state.

Now, notoriously, there are more than just *two* conflicting visions of Canada. For example, in his essay "English-Canadian Opposition to Quebec Nationalism," Andrew Stark describes four different "English-Canadian ideologies."[8] Journalist Jeffrey Simpson has identified no fewer than eight visions of Canada. He explores each through the biography and public accomplishments of a prominent Canadian.[9] So, in asserting that the Canadian political culture contains only two visions, we may seem to be denying the obvious. But we oppose neither Stark's nor Simpson's claims. We regard them as useful lists, and our aim is not to reduce or add to them. It is to examine a few specific conflicts that these visions generate and to ask whether shifting attention to an over-arching set of ground rules makes them look less intractable. To clarify this, let us distinguish more clearly between a vision and a meta-vision.

Differences over the appropriate approach to public policy are to be expected in a liberal democracy. There will always be debates over, for example, whether too strong a commitment to the welfare state creates a culture of dependency; how great a role the state should play in the economy; whether access to minority language services should be expanded or contracted; whether affirmative action programs are discriminatory; and so on. The conflicts between a number of the visions identified by Stark and Simpson are of this sort.[10] Such differences are not a bad thing in a liberal society. Indeed, kept within reasonable limits, they are a *good* thing. Liberal politics assume such differences. The liberal way to solve them is through debate, negotiation, elections or the courts.

However, this way of resolving differences assumes that the means employed — e.g., the use of the courts or of democratic debate in existing political institutions — rest upon principles that are widely shared in the community. This is crucial if the outcome of such decision-making processes is to have legitimacy, especially in the eyes of the losers. The really serious problem Canadians face is not that they have too many visions of their country. It is that some of these visions reflect more than just the usual disagreements over approaches to public policy. They reflect fundamental differences over how the political community should handle, or fairly adjudicate, such conflicting views.

This sort of disagreement is far more serious and divisive. The result is that essentially normal political disputes are often transformed into conflicts over the very nature of the roles and responsibilities of the two orders of government; the rules and procedures surrounding the democratic process; the legitimacy of key institutions; and the list and scope of the rights of citizens. Hence Canadians' notorious penchant for turning everything into a constitutional problem.

In a polity where such cleavages exist and become exposed, often not even a verdict from the highest court will resolve a serious dispute, for the courts themselves will likely be perceived as partial to a particular and controversial point of view. Insofar as that is the case, their decisions will often lack legitimacy in the eyes of the losers. More than once, court decisions have caused grief and anger in native communities for just this reason.[11] Similarly, many Quebec nationalists have regarded the Charter-based decisions of the Supreme Court that struck down sections of Bill 101 as illegitimate.[12] In sum, Canadians seem to disagree not only on their respective *visions* of the country — a normal occurrence in a liberal democracy — they also seem to disagree on what we have called the *meta-vision* that arches over it.

In one tradition — strong in Quebec, among some westerners and, in a less direct way, among some Aboriginal people[13] — a heavy emphasis is placed on the commitment to respect the diversity of the country through federalism.[14] In the other tradition, this commitment to diversity is seen as independent of, and subordinate to, the view that a liberal state's primary commitment is to protect and promote the freedom

14

and equality of citizens. We will call these viewpoints, respectively, the *federal point of view* and *traditional liberalism.*

Traditional liberalism subdivides into two camps: *classical* and *egalitarian.* The pan-Canadianism of the 1970s and 1980s draws inspiration from both: the former in terms of its commitment to the primacy of individual freedom and equality over diversity; the latter in terms of its commitment to use state power to promote equality of opportunity for all citizens. Before examining how this has affected the practice of Canadian federalism over the last quarter century, we must look briefly at the history of liberalism.

THREE FORMS OF LIBERALISM?

Liberalism is a dynamic tradition that has evolved and changed over the centuries. All liberals agree that the power of the state should be limited by a respect for individual freedom and equality. Nevertheless, there have been important disagreements over what this implies and how it is to be achieved. For the purposes of this book, we identify three broad divisions among liberal theorists.

"Classical" liberalism emerged in Europe from the religious wars of the 17th century. Liberal theorists of the day were preoccupied with questions of individual freedom, including the need for religious tolerance, guarantees of free speech and association, and the protection of private property. For classical liberals, rights are essentially "negative" – that is, they allow individuals to *prevent the state from interfering* with certain aspects of their personal freedom. Rights place a kind of fence around the individual, creating a "sphere of privacy" within which all individuals have an equal right to pursue their personal interests as they see fit. Classical liberals understand individual equality mainly in terms of the rule of law – that is, the state should accord everyone's freedom (defined in terms of these basic rights) the same respect.

In the 19th century, some liberals rejected the classical view of freedom. The plight of the working class convinced reformers that classical liberalism was inadequate. What good was, say, a legal right to freedom of speech to an ignorant and illiterate coal miner in 19th century England? In order to really exercise this liberty, reformers argued, such a person needed an opportunity to inform himself – say, by reading newspapers and discussing the issues of the day with his fellow citizens. Someone who is ignorant and illiterate may well have a right to speak, but what will he have to say?

Reformers showed that conditions necessary for the meaningful *exercise* of freedom go beyond "negative rights"; they also include access to certain basic social resources, such as education. Thus, reformers established a link between individual freedom and social equality. In their politics, they were quick to realize the implications of the new position: the liberal state must be more than just a *protector* of individual freedom; it must also be a *promoter* of it. Liberalism, according to this view, implicitly involves a commitment to social goals such as universal literacy and financial security. Individual liberty rights (e.g., the right to enjoy one's property and wealth unhindered) must therefore sometimes be weighed against the society's commitment to promoting social equality. Hence, reformers supplemented the negative rights of classical liberalism with a regime of "positive" rights. These "social" rights allowed individuals to enlist the power of the state in order to ensure that they received, say, a minimum level of education.

This "egalitarian" approach to liberal theory was thus based upon a commitment to promote "equality of opportunity," as opposed to the weaker "equality before the law" of classical liberalism. This laid the philosophical foundations for the modern welfare state as defended most influentially by John Rawls in *A Theory of Justice*.

In recent years, however, dissatisfaction with some of the arguments of egalitarian liberalism has given rise to what looks like a new, third phase of liberalism. During this century, particularly in the aftermath of World War II, both classical and egalitarian liberals have tended to regard membership in cultural and linguistic groups in much the same way as membership in religious groups – that is, as essentially a matter of private choice, an aspect of "civil society." As long as the existence of such groups does not impinge on personal liberty, they should be allowed to flourish. In this view, when the needs or interests of a cultural or linguistic community conflict with individual free choice, the state is wrong to act in ways that protect the interests of the community at the expense of individual freedom.[15]

If there is a new third wave emerging in liberal theory, it seems to be motivated by a growing conviction that community membership – especially in cultural and linguistic communities – involves more than just issues of private choice. Many liberals now agree that both human well-being and meaningful individual freedom require access to a range of values, goals, customs, practices and other "cultural goods." Such access is gained through membership in a healthy, developing cultural community. Equality of opportunity, in this view, extends beyond access to basic social goods such as education. It also includes a right to membership in a cultural or linguistic community.

Hence some liberals now argue that a respect for cultural and linguistic diversity is quite consistent with – perhaps even implied by – liberal commitments to individual freedom and equality. The establishment of this link ·between equality and community membership has given rise to a third form of liberal rights, so-called community rights. We will call this form of liberalism "cultural pluralism." It has been defended in different ways by a number of political theorists.[16]

Consider the example of francophone Quebecers who, under the Quebec Charter of the French Language (Bill 101), do not have the right to send their children to English-speaking schools. Some argue that this law violates basic liberal freedoms. But suppose it could be shown that the measure would reverse a trend in francophone society toward cultural fragmentation, a trend that might, if not reversed, disadvantage the members of that society in ways that would prevent them from meaningfully exercising their own freedom. In that case, a cultural pluralist such as Will Kymlicka, for example, would argue that preventing state action to assist the community, on the grounds that it would deprive some individuals of some measure of their individual freedom, only offends against the complementary liberal commitment to treat the interests of all citizens with equal concern and respect. The commitment to respect freedom must therefore be weighed against the commitment to respect equality.[17]

However, if cultural pluralism provides a basis for developing a liberal view of community rights that extends to cultural and linguistic minorities, it is indifferent to a third class of "community rights" that has been central to debates over Canadian federalism: *provincial rights*.[18] Liberal political theorist Allen Buchanan has provided a defence of "states' rights" in federal systems that sheds light on this issue.[19] He insists on the right of a state (or province) in a federal system to oppose what he calls *discriminatory redistribution*. This happens when a central government uses its powers to implement "taxation schemes or regulatory regimes or economic programs that *systematically work to the disadvantage of some groups, while benefiting others, in morally arbitrary ways*."[20]

According to Buchanan, individuals who share the same territory often develop strong economic links that integrate them into communities. The interests that underlie this kind of community membership are generally different from, but often

17

as important as, those attached to membership in a cultural or linguistic community. In regionally diverse countries such as Canada, the "national economy" contains a number of regions. They often operate on different cycles and have different economic and social interests. As a result, if one region has too much influence over the central government, it may be able to use this influence to promote policies that generally favour its interests over those of the others. This not only leads to an unfair distribution of the benefits of common membership, but also can directly interfere with provinces' attempts to develop policies aimed at promoting their own interests.

DIVERSITY *VS.* INDIVIDUAL FREEDOM AND EQUALITY

Our attempt to sketch a new meta-vision for Canadian federalism draws inspiration from the ideas and arguments of cultural pluralism and to some degree from Buchanan's analysis of discriminatory redistribution.

Cultural pluralism helps us to evaluate and respond to the claims of certain cultural and linguistic communities within Canada from a liberal point of view. In contrast to traditional liberalism, we claim that when the harm done to those individuals who lose some part of their unfettered right to, say, freedom of choice is minimal in comparison to the benefits that flow to those whose community is preserved or in some important way enhanced by the measure, it seems doctrinaire to insist that individual rights should simply "trump" the state's right to promote the interests of the community. Thus, if it can be convincingly shown that, say, the limitations placed on French-speaking Quebecers' right to freedom of choice as a result of Bill 101's restrictions on education is small relative to the gains for Quebec society as a whole, and if Quebecers democratically support the measures, the limitation placed on freedom of choice is justified.

The concept of discriminatory redistribution provides the basis for our view that federalism involves a special kind of respect for "regional communities." In line with post-war liberal egalitarianism generally, and pan-Canadianism in particular, we think the commitment to equality justifies the use of federal powers to redistribute wealth in order to promote equality of opportunity. Over the past 40 years the federal government has played a key role in developing and maintaining what has aptly been called the "sharing community."[21] We believe the federal government should continue to play the role of the principal agent of interprovincial equity. In particular, we regard equalization as a fundamental component of Canadian federalism.[22] A vision of federalism that puts too much emphasis on the liberal commitment to promote equality of opportunity will tend to make its supporters insensitive to the need to strike such a balance. This loads the dice in favour of centralization, as the goal of promoting greater equality for all Canadians will always trump provincial interests that conflict with it. Wherever there is inequality, the federal government will be able to claim a right – a *duty* – to take action to promote equality, even when this interferes with legitimate attempts by provincial governments to promote their own objectives.

In a country as vast as Canada, however, inequalities of opportunity abound. A "just" reason for the creation of new federal regulatory schemes and social programs in areas of provincial jurisdiction can thus always be found. If a better balance is to be struck, Canadians must accept that a province's demand that its diversity be respected sometimes imposes limits on the federal right to promote national equality.[23]

At bottom, our position thus differs from orthodox liberalism in that it rejects the claim that a committed liberal must distinguish the respect for certain forms of diversity from, and subordinate it to, the respect for individual freedom and equality. We regard these as parallel commitments.[24] We are not denying liberals' claim that Canadians should respect liberal-democratic values and principles. The difference between our view and that of traditional liberals lies not in whether we share the commitment that the state's primary aim is to promote the freedom and equality of all individuals – we do. Rather, it lies in how we understand the limitations that the commitment to federalism can legitimately place upon both (negative) liberal rights and upon the right of the central government to act positively to promote the pan-Canadian goal of equality of opportunity.

Notes

1. P.B. Waite (ed.), *The Confederation Debates in the Province of Canada/1865* (Toronto: McClelland and Stewart Ltd., 1963), p. 58.

2. Waite (ed.), *The Confederation Debates*, p. 74.

3. Waite (ed.), *The Confederation Debates*, p. 40.

4. These measures included the powers of reservation and disallowance, the peace, order and good government clause, and the fact that Senators, lieutenant governors and superior court judges would be appointed by the Governor General in Council.

5. The phrase was coined by K.C. Wheare in *Federal Government* (London: Oxford University Press, 1946).

6. On the Privy Council's tendency to seek a balance between provincial autonomy and federal power in the first century after Confederation, see Peter Russell, "Introduction," in Peter Russell, Rainer Knopff and Ted Morton (eds.), *Federalism and the Charter: Leading Constitutional Decisions* (Ottawa: Carleton University Press, 1989), pp. 5-14.

7. For a similar point of view, see F.L. Morton, "Group Rights Versus Individual Rights in the Charter: The Special Cases of Natives and the *Québécois*," in Neil Nevitte and Allan Kornberg (eds.), *Minorities and the Canadian State* (Oakville, Ontario: Mosaic Press, 1985), pp. 72, 77-84.

8. These are the visions of Pierre Trudeau, English-Canadian nationalism in its current social democratic form, the Western Reform movement and some of the doctrines developing around the Charter of Rights and Freedoms. See Andrew Stark, "English-Canadian Opposition to Quebec Nationalism," in Kent Weaver (ed.), *The Collapse of Canada?* (Washington: Brookings Institution, 1992), p. 123.

9. These individuals are Derek Burney, Mary Eberts, Preston Manning, Clyde Wells, George Erasmus, Joe Fratesi, Lucien Bouchard and Léon Dion. See Jeffrey Simpson, *Faultlines: Struggling for a Canadian Vision* (Toronto: HarperCollins, 1993).

10. For example, many of the differences in the visions of Mary Eberts, Clyde Wells, Joe Fratesi

and Preston Manning that are described in Jeffrey Simpson's *Faultlines* fall more or less into this category.

11. A recent example occurred in 1991 when Chief Justice Allan MacEachern of the BC Supreme Court dismissed a land claim made by the Gitksan Wet'suwet'en Indians. Native leaders insisted that Justice MacEachern's decision reflected "Eurocentric" views. They subsequently appealed to the United Nations Human Rights Commission to review this decision. The UN report, released on April 1, 1993, agreed with the Gitksan. According to the report, the judge's ruling was proof that "deeply rooted Western ethnocentric criteria are still widely shared in present-day judiciary reasoning." (See *The Globe and Mail*, April 2, 1993.)

12. It should be noted that in at least one of these decisions, the *Ford* decision on signage, it was concluded that the measure conflicted with Quebec's own charter of rights. See *Ford v. Quebec (A.G.)* [1988] 2 S.C.R. 712.

13. This connection, perhaps not obvious at first blush, will be explained in later chapters.

14. See Alain-G. Gagnon and François Rocher, "Faire l'histoire au lieu de la subir," in Alain-G. Gagnon and François Rocher (eds.), *Répliques aux détracteurs de la souveraineté du Québec* (Montréal: vlb éditeur, 1992), p. 29.

15. For an argument that restrictive language laws violate liberal principles, see Ian Macdonald, "Group Rights," in *Philosophical Papers*, Vol. 28, no. 2 (1989), pp. 117-36.

16. Examples are Will Kymlicka, *Liberalism, Community and Culture* (Oxford: Clarendon Press, 1989); Charles Taylor, "The Politics of Recognition," in Amy Gutmann (ed.), *Multiculturalism and "The Politics of Recognition"* (Princeton: Princeton University Press, 1992). Also, for a collection of essays assessing collective rights from a number of points of view, see Michael McDonald (ed.), *The Canadian Journal of Law and Jurisprudence*, Vol. 4, no. 2 (1992).

17. See Will Kymlicka, *Multicultural Citizenship: A Liberal Theory of Minority Rights* (Oxford University Press, forthcoming), chaps. 5, 6.

18. This is not quite right. Cultural pluralism has implications for provincial rights insofar as the rights at issue are linguistic or cultural. In the case of Quebec, for example, one might use a cultural pluralist argument to defend claims to certain powers for the National Assembly.

19. Allen Buchanan, *Secession: The Morality of Political Divorce from Fort Sumpter to Lithuania and Quebec* (Boulder: Westview Press, 1991), pp. 38-45.

20. Buchanan, *Secession*, p. 40 (italics in original).

21. See Peter M. Leslie, "The Fiscal Crisis of Canadian Federalism," in *A Partnership in Trouble: Renegotiating Fiscal Federalism* (Toronto: C.D. Howe Institute, 1993), pp. 5-9.

22. That is not to say that we accept the *status quo* regarding the entire system of redistribution.

23. This is further discussed in chapter 4 of this volume.

24. For an argument that equality cannot be reconciled with diversity, see Morton, "Group Rights Versus Individual Rights in the Charter," pp. 71-85.

3

TRADITIONAL LIBERALISM AND THE FEDERAL POINT OF VIEW

As far as national unity goes, up until the first century after Confederation the Canadian synthesis of liberalism and federalism worked well enough. Certainly, there were crises, such as the one over conscription in 1942, but the country was not lurching from one national unity crisis to another, as it seems to have done over the last three decades. One reason the synthesis seems to have worked is that for the first century federalism was the principal philosophical base of our constitutional politics.

While the 1867 Constitution spelled out the commitment to federalism in some detail, it lacked any equivalent of the American Bill of Rights. There was little in the written Constitution that could count as an authoritative statement of Canadians' commitment to liberalism. If liberalism is the view that government should be limited by a respect for individual freedom, there was remarkably little in the British North America Act about what those freedoms were in Canadian society. Liberalism was, of course, embedded in our common law inheritance from Britain and in our unwritten constitution as well as within the political tradition of parliamentary government; but the lack of a bill of rights meant that Parliament and the legislatures were supreme in their respective fields.[1]

There were disadvantages and advantages to this. From the point of view of individual freedom, the absence of an entrenched bill of rights meant Canadians' commitment to liberalism was not well defined and hence relatively easy to ignore.[2] From the point of view of policy makers, it helped keep out of the public consciousness the natural tensions between, on the one hand, the liberal commitment to freedom and equality and, on the other, the federalist one to respecting diversity. For the first century after Confederation, liberalism thus remained a flexible doctrine the interpretation of which could be changed to suit the needs of the country and the times. A spectacular example of this occurred in the post-war period.

Before the war, the view of liberalism that dominated policy making in Canada was essentially a classical one with the emphasis on individual freedom and free market economics. In practice, liberal equality was largely understood to mean a commitment to the rule of law. The idea that "meaningful participation" in a liberal society might require Canadians to see equality as implying a range of "social rights" never really caught on until the post-war period.[3] As a result of the Depression, social rights had been discussed fairly widely in the 1930s, particularly by the Co-operative Commonwealth Federation (CCF). The Liberals, under Prime Minister Mackenzie King, had committed themselves to a "socially conscious Canada" in the 1935 election. There had even been some significant policy initiatives, such as Prime Minister R.B. Bennett's New Deal legislation. Still, most of this was talk. The vision of classical liberalism remained the dominant force. The real policy revolution was yet to come.

With the arrival of Keynesian economics, governments suddenly had an economic theory that was not only compatible with, but encouraged, the adoption of the egalitarian language of social rights. If the cyclical periods of economic contraction and high unemployment could be avoided by government spending, continuous growth and full employment would be more or less assured. Activist government came into its own. What the establishment had been wary of a decade earlier quickly became the new orthodoxy of policy makers and intellectuals as governments threw themselves into the task of building the welfare state.[4]

In sum, the absence of any equivalent of the American Bill of Rights meant that questions ranging from limits on free speech, sexual equality and the mobility of citizens to the extent of citizens' social entitlements were regarded as essentially political or legal ones – that is, as a prerogative of Parliament and the legislatures. When the two orders of government differed on such issues, the traditional system of accommodation could be relied upon to resolve the impasse through negotiation, by finding a political solution. Insofar as policy makers were subject to constitutional constraints, from the point of view of the courts these had mainly to do with technical matters about the jurisdictional limits placed on governments by the distribution of powers.

TRADITIONAL LIBERALISM AND THE CHARTER

The passage of Prime Minister Diefenbaker's Bill of Rights in 1960 marks the beginning of a change in the role of liberalism in Canadian political culture. But that law, only a federal statute, did not bind the provinces and could be changed at the whim of Parliament. In the constitutional rounds that followed, entrenchment of a charter of rights was discussed. When the Constitution was finally patriated in 1982, it included such a charter.

The entrenchment of the Charter of Rights and Freedoms fundamentally altered the relationship between liberalism and federalism.[5] It gave liberalism a new legal standing and a new kind of moral authority among the people. In general, the project of bringing Canadians' commitment to liberalism out of the shadows of their political culture so that it could be clearly seen and inspected by the public eye was a good and important one. Ideally, this change would have happened in circumstances that better allowed Canadians to adjust to the new official status that the Charter, with its emphasis on freedom, equality and the rights of the individual, gave to both classical and egalitarian liberalism. Ideally, too, it would have allowed us to find new ways to integrate liberalism with the existing commitment to federalism, i.e., the respect for diversity.

This is not what happened. The Charter, presented by Prime Minister Trudeau to the Canadian public as "the people's package," spawned a new Canadian political discourse based on an egalitarian approach to individual liberal rights.[6] On a number of issues, the logic of this discourse has come into direct collision with the views of those who, having adopted a more federalist point of view, advocated a more decentralized, a more culturally pluralistic or a more regionally representative, form of federalism.

The result has been an ongoing battle over the "real meaning" of the country's twin commitments to federalism and liberalism, as spokespersons on all sides struggle to legitimize their own vision in the eyes of the Canadian public. This has been especially intense on two fronts. One concerns the limits of liberal individual rights; the other the promotion of economic and social equality. We now wish to take a closer look at three points where these conflicts have been most clearly focussed: in Quebec, among Aboriginal peoples and in the West.

FEDERALISM AND THE LANGUAGE OF SOVEREIGNTY

In Quebec, what we will call "the language of sovereignty" has led to the development of a political vocabulary that sometimes seems incomprehensible to people in English-speaking Canada. In particular, terms such as the "distinct society," "sovereignty-association" and "cultural sovereignty" leave some in the rest of Canada wondering what is being said. The logic of this position has its origin in a particular conception of "the nation" and "sovereignty." In a liberal-democratic state it is "the people" who are sovereign. However, Canada is sociologically diverse. Indeed, some insist that it is a multinational state.[7] In practice, the phrases "the people" and "the nation" have always been understood from more than one point of view. Depending on which one is adopted, both the meaning and the moral sense of the "national" or "common" interest can differ profoundly. The "masters in our own house" slogan, first used by Maurice Duplessis and later picked up by Jean Lesage, brilliantly exploited this ambiguity. Among Quebecers, its use effectively drove a wedge between two very different senses of "the nation" in Canadian political discourse: that of Canada as a whole and that of French-speaking Quebecers.[8]

The claim that Quebecers were not already "masters" in their "own home" could be understood on two levels. First, it could be taken to mean that Quebec is not simply a "region," "province" or other subunit of the federation like all the others. It is the "home" of French-speaking Canadians as a cultural community. This is the basis for Lesage's claim that Confederation was a pact between two founding peoples and that Quebec has a special status within it.[9] However, the idea of being "masters" in this "home," if rigorously adhered to, evokes the broader idea (opposed by Lesage) of a right to a "homeland" or nation-state that would be the political expression of Quebecers' status as a sovereign people. This was the interpretation given to the slogan by *indépendantistes*. It not only denied the federal government's right to exercise certain powers, but also implicitly challenged the consensus around which the very language of federalism (and of our national politics) had been built, namely that there exists a common Canadian interest the federal government should promote.

According to this critique, the federalist point of view presupposes a level of consensus on basic aims, values and interests which, according to *indépendantistes*, the Canadian political community lacks. In particular, they say the interests, aims and values of Quebec society often conflict with those of the rest of Canada. To find the kind of consensus presupposed by the federalist point of view, we must, in their view, descend to the level of subgroups within Confederation. In Quebec (continues the argument), the significant degree of cultural and linguistic homogeneity allows such a consensus on broad public policy issues to form. There, the idea of a "common" or "national" interest is a reality rather than a myth. Canada as a whole (they conclude) is sociologically too diverse to expect a really substantive consensus to be forged around the idea of a "common interest."

The Lesage slogan thus turned out to be more than a rallying point for French-speaking Quebecers, as that premier had intended. In the end, it provided the independence movement with powerful sociological and theoretical arguments for rejecting the very foundations of the federalist point of view.

The introduction of the Charter can be seen in this context as the liberal reply to the *indépendantistes*. By linking the idea of Canadian citizenship more directly to individual rights, the Charter placed new – and substantive – limits on how the common Canadian interest could be defined.[10] From the point of view of traditional liberalism, "the nation" is first and foremost a voluntary association of *free and equal* individuals. The idea of the common interest is therefore not to be defined in terms of some vague notion of shared values and aims resulting from a shared culture and language, as the *indépendantistes* maintain, but by what will preserve and promote the freedom and equality of all citizens. Whether or not they share a common cultural or linguistic background is incidental.

In effect, then, the Charter, insofar as it was thought to reflect a pan-Canadian conception of citizenship, appeared as a denial of *indépendantistes'* key claim that Canada's sociological diversity impairs Canadians' ability to arrive at a substantive definition of their common interests. By raising the profile of the traditional liberal view that just states are based on a respect for individual freedom and equality, the Charter became a powerful rejoinder to the *indépendantistes'* attempt to co-opt the language of the liberal nation-state and turn it against the Canadian federation.[11]

In general, this strategy of clarifying and raising the profile of Canadians' shared commitment to freedom and equality is both laudable and a legitimate reply to *indépendantistes*. The respect for individual freedom and equality is a basic commitment for all Canadians. However, the pan-Canadian vision that inspired this counter-offensive did so by clearly subordinating the federal point of view to the assumptions of classical liberalism. This has at least two unacceptable consequences.

First, it implicitly denies the validity of moderate nationalists' claim that, as the only province with a French-speaking majority, the Quebec government has a special mission in Confederation. Here the classical liberal view of the equality of citizens, which underwrites pan-Canadianism, prevents those who adopt a pan-Canadian approach from doing justice to the commitment to respect diversity.

Second, it implies that considerations of shared culture, language or history are of marginal concern, if not irrelevant, to what the Canadian Charter, in section 1, calls the "reasonable limits" that can be placed on rights "in a free and democratic society." This insistence that the moral foundations of the state can and ought to be kept neutral in such matters, however noble in theory, leads in practice to a doctrinaire conception of freedom and equality in general and of the rights set out in the Charter in particular.

FEDERALISM AND THE LANGUAGE OF COLONIALISM

The second point of conflict between liberalism and federalism involves Aboriginal people and stems from what we will call "the language of colonialism." In recent years, First Nations have begun to assert themselves as independent players on the national stage, demanding constitutional recognition of their "historical rights" as self-governing peoples. Having succeeded in obtaining recognition of their "existing rights" in the 1982 Constitution, they refocussed their efforts on trying to get those rights more clearly defined. At the same time, they have argued for a constitutional recognition of their undefined "inherent right to self-government."

During the Canada Round, an acrimonious debate broke out over the relationship between the inherent right to self-government and liberal democracy. Most native groups were not only willing but wanted to see their governments remain within the Canadian federal state.[12] Federalism, as some pointed out, is among the traditional forms of government practised by some North American Indians. The Iroquois Confederacy, for example, was praised by Ben Franklin and considered as a model for the thirteen colonies.[13] However, if there was strong support for federalism among native leaders, there was serious disagreement over the question of whether, or how far, self-government should be subject to the Charter.

On the one hand, many non-native Canadians and the Native Women's Association of Canada argued that the Charter should apply, and in the same way, to all Canadians. On the other hand, some native leaders, such as Chief Ovide

Mercredi of the Assembly of First Nations, argued that doing so would undermine traditional ways of life in some Indian communities. The concentration on individual rights, they insisted, was foreign and, in some cases, even contrary to the traditional practices and values of many native communities. Attempting to superimpose "Eurocentric values" on them would be just another way of maintaining the "colonial relationship" from which they are seeking release. Self-government is meaningless, it was said, if it does not allow Indian peoples to preserve their distinct cultures and traditional ways of life – even though these sometimes conflict with the liberal-democratic institutions and values that non-native Canadians have imported from Europe.

In our view, a commitment to the respect for basic liberal rights must be viewed as a background condition for the development of any just society. Nevertheless, we also maintain that such respect is compatible with interpretations of the meanings of those rights which may diverge in important ways. Thus, while there would be nothing "Eurocentric" about making respect for human rights a condition of Aboriginal self-government, there might well be something "Eurocentric" about demanding that the Canadian Charter apply to that self-government in the same way that it applies to, say, British Columbians.

But subordinating the respect for diversity to equality, as under traditional liberalism, has precisely this consequence; for it supports a pan-Canadian or universalist view of citizenship. By contrast, we maintain that a differential application of rights is not ruled out by the commitment to equality. In this view, it is quite possible that the courts might from time to time conclude that an appeal to the commitment to respect diversity constitutes a "reasonable limit" (as provided in section 1 of the Charter) on the exercise of a right within one community but not another.

Thus, one could imagine the courts taking a non-standard view of how the democratic rights in the Charter were to be applied in a self-governing Mohawk community, on the grounds that some special limitation was called for in order to protect the community's traditional leadership selection practices. Accepting such limitations does *not* necessarily amount to giving different citizens different rights in a manner that conflicts with the Charter; nor does it mean that the right is not being applied to all citizens. It simply means that a cultural community's collective will to preserve its heritage can *sometimes* count as a "reasonable limit" on individual freedoms. Equality of treatment, in short, does not always require sameness of treatment.

FEDERALISM AND THE LANGUAGE OF ALIENATION

The third critical area of conflict between the pan-Canadian vision and federalism can be found in the West, and stems from what we call "the language of alienation." Over the years, the four western provinces, led by Alberta, have forcefully articulated a critique of Confederation as a political arrangement designed to serve the interests of "Central Canada" (i.e., Ontario and Quebec). This has led to the development of a political culture in the West that views Westerners as "outsiders" who are alienated from the political establishment in Central Canada.

In this view, decision making in the federal Parliament is (more or less) based upon the principle of representation by population ("rep-by-pop"): one person, one vote. This principle reflects the liberal commitment to the equality of citizens. Given its large share of the population, Central Canada has a majority of seats in the House of Commons and thus the power to pass or reject most legislation. Moreover, responsible government and party discipline have had the effect of concentrating decision-making power – in this case, in the hands of the Prime Minister and a small coterie of senior ministers. According to Westerners, however, this inner circle traditionally has been dominated by Central Canada. This combination of "rep-by-pop" and responsible government, they claim, has given Central Canada enormous influence in national decision making. In their view, the result is that federal policy has systematically favoured the interests of the centre over those of the periphery.[14]

For those who view Confederation this way, the redistributive language of egalitarian liberalism is often little more than a smokescreen to justify policies that reflect the interests and priorities of the Prime Minister and the Cabinet. The real problem with Canadian federalism, they conclude, is that it makes the federalist idea of "the national" or "common Canadian" interest simply a prerogative of the federal executive, which is controlled by Central Canada and has the power to define it by *fiat*. Over time, say Westerners, such an arrangement is bound to favour the centre. The resulting (re)distribution of goods and opportunities discriminates against the West as a region.

Westerners maintain that, in a federal system where regional interests were fairly taken into account, the executive would have to *negotiate* the legislative agenda that embodied its conception of the "national interest" with an independent body of credible regional representatives. Such a regional component could, in their view, be incorporated into the federal decision-making process in various ways, such as, for example, a popularly elected Senate with satisfactorily balanced regional representation.[15]

In this view, then, federalism is a system of government that is designed to balance the protection of regional interests with the commitment to respect citizen equality. Since Canada is a liberal-democratic, federal state, conclude Westerners, its Parliament should have one house (the Commons) based upon "rep-by-pop" and one based upon "rep-by-region" (or by province). Our present liberal commitment to individual equality would then be balanced by our federalist commitment to provide adequate protection to the less populous provinces.

Insofar as this account accurately reflects what can be called the "Western point of view," its defenders are critical of at least two aspects of the pan-Canadian vision of Canadian federalism. First, there is considerable suspicion of the kind of federal activism that the redistributive language of egalitarian liberalism has sometimes been used to justify.[16] Second, as many Westerners see it, pan-Canadianism puts too heavy an emphasis on citizen equality, with the result that the particular interests of regional communities are not well protected. In response, many Westerners have become staunch defenders of the so-called principle of the equality of provinces.

This "principle" of federalism is advanced as a complement to the equality of citizens. Westerners have used it as a fulcrum on which to lever their case for stronger regional representation to offset what is perceived to be the Central Canadian bias of pan-Canadianism. Their argument was given additional force by the fact that, as the champion of pan-Canadianism, Prime Minister Trudeau's own account of the relation between liberalism and federalism relies heavily on the principle. He has always maintained that liberal equality is incompatible with a "special status" or "differential rights" for any province – notably Quebec. Trudeau also appeared implicitly to recognize the principle in the amending formula of the Constitution. The requirement of unanimity for certain purposes means no distinction is in this respect acknowledged between the decision-making weight of, say, Prince Edward Island and Ontario.[17]

Notes

1. In 1867 the supremacy of Parliament was subject to the Governor General's power to reserve a bill "for the signification of the Queen's pleasure" and to possible disallowance by the British government. The supremacy of a legislature was subject to parallel reservation and disallowance at the federal level. These powers have fallen into disuse and according to many can no longer be invoked.

2. Examples include the failure to grant women and status Indians the vote and the head tax placed upon Chinese immigrants.

3. Social rights aim at the satisfaction of basic needs (e.g., through welfare, old age pensions and health care) or to ensure equality of opportunity (e.g., through worker training or education).

4. Robert Campbell, *Grand Illusions: The Politics of the Keynesian Experience in Canada 1945-1975* (Toronto: Broadview Press, 1987), pp. 3-35.

5. See Alan Cairns, *Charter vs. Federalism: The Dilemma of Constitutional Reform* (Montreal and Kingston: McGill-Queen's University Press, 1992), especially pp. 33-61; David Milne, "Canada's Constitutional Odyssey," in Michael Whittington and Glen Williams (eds.), *Canadian Politics in the 1990s*, 3rd ed. (Scarborough: Nelson Canada, 1990), pp. 213-35; David Shugarman, "Ideology and the Charter," in David Shugarman and Reg Whitaker (eds.), *Federalism and Political Community* (Toronto: Broadview Press, 1989), pp. 307-25.

6. A good summary of this can be found in Jeffrey Simpson, *Faultlines: Struggling for a Canadian Vision* (Toronto: HarperCollins, 1993), pp. 65-107.

7. See Philip Resnick, "Toward a Multinational Federalism: Asymmetrical and Confederal Alternatives," in F. Leslie Seidle (ed.), *Seeking a New Canadian Partnership: Asymmetrical and Confederal Options* (Montreal: Institute for Research on Public Policy, 1994), p. 86.

8. In fact, the situation was more complicated than this because the expression "the nation" as traditionally used by French-speaking nationalists referred to *les Canadiens français*, not just French-speaking *Quebecers*. See below, chap. 8.

9. The "compact theory of Confederation" in fact goes back many years. For example, in 1925 the then Minister of Justice, Ernest Lapointe, in a speech in the House of Commons, referred to Confederation as a pact between four provinces, while discussing a proposed amendment to the British North America Act. He also quoted Wilfrid Laurier, speaking in 1907, to the same effect. See MacGregor Dawson, *Constitutional Issues in Canada 1900 - 1933* (Toronto: Oxford University Press, 1933), pp. 14-18.

10. Section 36 of the Constitution Act, 1982 should also be borne in mind here. It commits the federal and provincial governments to work together to establish equality of opportunity, reduce economic disparity and provide essential public services to all citizens.

11. That is, of free and equal citizens who share a common cultural and linguistic background (i.e., a *nation*) joining together to found a nation-state in which to determine their own destiny. This view has deep roots in liberal theory. According to J.S. Mill, for example, "Free institutions are next to impossible in a country made up of different nationalities. Among a people with fellow-feeling, especially if they read and speak different languages, the united public opinion, necessary to the working of representative government, cannot exist...[I]t is in general a necessary condition of free institutions that the boundaries of governments should coincide in the main with those of nationalities." John Stuart Mill, *Considerations on Representative Government* (Indianapolis: Bobbs-Merrill, 1958), pp. 230-31.

12. Given that they were seeking the creation of a *third* order of government, independent of the other two, one might question whether they accepted *federalism* at all. Traditionally, federalism is based upon a division between *two* levels of government. But debating this probably only comes down to fighting over how to use the word "federalism" and need not concern us here.

13. Edmond Orban, *Fédéralisme: Super état fédéral? Association d'états souverains?* (Montreal: HMH Ltee., 1992), pp. 25-35.

14. One might want to expand this to include not only people in the western provinces, but also in the four Atlantic ones and even the territories. Some therefore now speak of "Outer Canada" to underline that there is a general sense of alienation felt by people on the periphery toward the centre.

15. For some thoughts along these lines, see Gordon Robertson, *A House Divided: Meech Lake, Senate Reform and the Canadian Union* (Halifax: Institute for Research on Public Policy, 1989), pp. 1-9, 65-72; and Douglas Verney, "Incorporating Canada's Other Political Tradition," in Shugarman and Whitaker (eds.), *Federalism and Political Community*, pp. 187-202.

16. It may be necessary to distinguish the far West – i.e., Alberta and British Columbia, both of which are "have" provinces – from Manitoba and Saskatchewan, both "have not" provinces that depend upon the federal transfer system. Still, we should bear in mind the period in the late 1970s when Saskatchewan became for a time a "have" province. During that period, the Saskatchewan government emerged as a strong and articulate defender of provincial rights. However, with the crash in world prices for natural resources and agricultural products, this period of relative prosperity came to an end. The province was markedly less provincialist during the 1980s under Conservative Premier Grant Devine.

17. The formulae in Part V of the Constitution Act, 1982, were not, however, Trudeau's first preference. He proposed the "Victoria formula" of 1971, which was not based on equality of the provinces but gave a veto to each of Ontario and Quebec. Trudeau conceded equality only when it was clear in 1981 that no other formula could gain acceptance.

4

PAN-CANADIANISM
AND THE
NATION-BUILDING PROJECT

The commitment to respect diversity through federalism is about accommodating different kinds of *communities* in a single state. Hence, the British North America Act, with its emphasis on federalism, was concentrated on defining the relationship between governments. By contrast, liberalism is about respect for *individual* freedom and equality through limited government. Insofar as the Charter is a liberal document, its purpose was to clarify Canadians' view of the relationship between citizen and state.

This was an important task. It was important not only because individual rights merit constitutional protection, but also because the creation of the Charter looked like a reasonable way to further the project of nation building. It would make both official language communities feel at home anywhere in Canada, ensure greater cohesion among governments in policy making, enhance mobility, serve as a symbol of Canadian unity and generally reduce the risk of political and social conflict. However, to many French-speaking Quebecers and some Aboriginal people, the Charter appeared instead as an instrument of assimilation into what, in their eyes, is largely the culture of English-speaking Canada.

This critique of the Charter is unjustified. However, the dominant view of the Charter in English-speaking Canada has been, and remains, one that reflects the pan-Canadian vision of its chief architect, Pierre Trudeau. His approach to Charter interpretation defines individual rights in a way that seems unduly antagonistic to the spirit of federalism. Trudeau recognizes that Canadians' twin commitments to liberalism and federalism stem from different sets of interests – namely, their interest in, on the one hand, freedom and equality and, on the other, community member-ship. But he insists that in a liberal society the freedom and equality of individuals must prevail over the rights of communities. We think this pan-Canadian approach misrepresents the nature of the Charter in particular and of liberal-democratic rights in general.

Two Approaches to the Charter

Section 1 of the Charter states that Charter rights can be limited by such "reasonable limits" as can be justified in a "free and democratic society." For Trudeau, this means they should be infringed only "by the necessity of also guaranteeing their exercise to other members of the society."[1] Consistent with liberal egalitarian prin-ciples, he argues against the view of classical liberals that, in practice, negative rights may legitimately be limited by positive government action, when such action is required to ensure that all citizens have an equal opportunity to exercise basic rights. As he puts it: "[W]here is the justice in a country in which an individual has the freedom to be totally fulfilled, but where inequality denies him the means?"[2]

In general, we have no quarrel with this line of argument. But we think Trudeau fails in his attempt to preempt parallel arguments advanced by cultural pluralists. They maintain that basic rights may sometimes be infringed in order to protect the collective interests of certain linguistic and cultural groups. Trudeau replies that, in his view, it is of the essence of liberalism that:

> [A]ll members of a civil society enjoy certain fundamental, inalienable rights and cannot be deprived of them by any collectivity (state or government) or on behalf of any collectivity (nation, ethnic group, religious group or other)... [O]nly the individual is the possessor of rights. A collectivity can exercise only those rights it has received by delegation from its members...[3]

The unspoken assumption here is that there is a relatively objective, and there-fore uncontroversial, way of distinguishing between the collective interests of com-munities and the individual's interest in freedom and equality such that the former can be subordinated to the latter.

In our view, this assumes a degree of consensus on Canadians' views about their community-based interests in language and culture that simply does not exist. This is evident from the debates over language law in Quebec and official bilingualism in the rest of Canada. In developing the Charter, Trudeau presumably hoped that by providing Canadians with an official political philosophy, their political institutions would eventually forge a consensus around it. This is the assumption behind classical nation-building strategies. But is it warranted here? On what grounds did Trudeau base this hope? The answer seems to lie in his personal commitment to the rationalistic philosophy of the European Enlightenment.

The *philosophes* of the French Enlightenment pictured human beings as, in their purest essence, autonomous rational moral agents. This vision inspired both the Declaration of the Rights of Man in 1789 and the American Bill of Rights in 1791. In similar vein, Trudeau tells us that in conceiving the Charter he pictured individuals as:

> ..."human personalities"...beings of a moral order – that is, free and equal among themselves, each having absolute dignity and infinite value. As such, they transcend the accidents of place and time, and partake in the essence of universal Humanity.[4]

This is a lofty, impressive and inspiring picture. By erasing from our view all of the "accidents of place and time" it encourages us to rise above the tribal instincts and deeply rooted cultural prejudices that still infect even the most liberal and democratic of societies. It is thus a picture that commits us to strive toward the deepest possible respect for individual autonomy; to found our society on a respect for the freedom and equality of all persons.

We certainly do not want to undermine or reject this point of view. Nevertheless, as a picture of human beings, the image is also abstract and overly intellectual. As such, we are inclined to regard it as one-sided. Whatever they may say about freedom and equality, when most people think about their dignity as individual persons, they usually think about what makes them the actual persons they are: their goals, values, beliefs, the life they share with their family, friends and colleagues, their accomplishments in art, science, sports, politics and so on. All of these, however, are inseparable from their place in a community, or a series of communities, of which they are members. Significantly, these aspects of our individual life and their connection with our membership in various communities appear as an afterthought in Trudeau's vision of moral individuals as "human personalities."

In our view, if Charter interpretation is to begin with an idealized picture of the "human personality," that picture must be broadened to include the fact of *belonging* to various communities as an essential part of the "human personality." And, indeed, there is a whole movement in modern philosophy that, on just this point, has argued against the one-sidedness of the European rationalistic tradition of the Enlightenment. In this alternative tradition, human persons are thought to identify with various communities in ways that make it impossible to distinguish clearly something called their "essential humanity" from something else called their "cultural and ancestral history." In Charles Taylor's words:

[O]ne cannot be a self on one's own. I am a self only in relation to certain interlocutors: in one way in relation to those conversation partners who were essential to my achieving self-definition; in another in relation to those who are now crucial to my continuing grasp of languages of self-understanding... The full definition of someone's identity thus usually involves not only his stand on moral and spiritual matters but also some reference to a defining community.[5]

Northrop Frye comes to a similar conclusion in his classic work *The Great Code: The Bible and Literature:*

This relation of society to individual corresponds to certain elements of ordinary life: we belong to something before we are anything, and we have entered a specific social contract before birth. I was predestined to be, for example, a middle-class mid-twentieth-century male white English-speaking Canadian in the instant of conception. But as the individual develops within his society, all the essential aspects of thought and imagination and experience take place in him. Social freedom, however essential, is general and approximate; real freedom is something that only the individual can experience. The individual grows out of society like a plant out of its soil; but he does not break away from it...[6]

There are thus two opposing views of human nature here. In one, the capacity for free choice and membership in, say, a cultural community are like two poles on a continuum. In this view, the task of balancing competing rights claims, or of deciding what constitutes a reasonable limit on the exercise of a right, turns on a close consideration of the social, cultural and historical values of the society: rights must be *contextualized*. These values provide the over-arching framework for drawing the line between individual freedom and community interest. The issue of where, exactly, "individuality" stops and "membership in the community" starts is thus essentially a social-cultural question.

In the second view of human nature, freedom is the human capacity for rational choice. To protect human freedom is to prevent the state from interfering with citizens' attempts to reflect on public and private matters and to act as their reason dictates. Because reason is a *human* capacity, it is transcultural. This suggests that the exercise of free thought must be more clearly distinguishable from membership in a particular community than the above model suggests. This view thus leans away from a strong emphasis on the need to contextualize rights and toward a universalistic approach to applying them.

In both views, the task of a charter and the *raison d'être* of liberalism are the same: to establish citizens' rights to individual freedom and equality and to protect citizens from domination by the collectivity. However, the two views differ in their understanding of the relation between individual and collectivity. As a result, when it comes to analyzing a particular case, the two models can lead to quite different conclusions. We think Trudeau's pan-Canadian approach to interpreting the Charter relies too heavily on a rationalistic view of human nature. It is not sensitive enough to the need to contextualize rights.

THE TASK OF CONTEXTUALIZING CHARTER RIGHTS

Insofar as there is a transcultural rational core to human freedom, the more clearly we understand the logic of the rights that define it, the less dependent Charter interpretation will be on contextualization and the more it will become an essentially technical task of applying the logic of these rights to a given situation. We do not deny that there are important generalizations that can be made about freedom and basic rights. Nevertheless, we believe the logic of human freedom is far less structured and far more richly textured than the rationalistic model suggests.

Freedom and equality mean many things to many people. When we examine how individuals or societies actually conceive of freedom, we find that it is defined in terms of their capacity to attain certain goals and objectives, to cultivate certain values and to live by certain principles, all of which reflect their own historical and cultural experiences. This is not to say that culturally inherited values and goals should be regarded as beyond question, but that for the individuals who pursue them, freedom is much more than just the abstract capacity or the political right to engage in such questioning – negative rights. Real freedom – *positive* freedom – is an achievement. It lies in the *attainment* of selected goals, the *cultivation* of cherished values and the *commitment* to chosen principles.

The question of where the individual's capacity to choose stops and membership in a community starts is an important one. In a relatively self-contained and culturally homogeneous society, it might be possible to draw clear lines. Where a strong underlying consensus exists around the norms of political and social life, citizens will have an intuitive sense of the limits of fairness, respect and legitimacy within their community. One simply "knows" what they are, how they work and, broadly speaking, what sorts of claims, objectives and policies are consistent with them.

However, the political culture in Canada has never had this kind of unity: that, as we noted, is why the Fathers opted for federalism in the first place. Subgroups within states such as Canada are often defined precisely by their different social, cultural and historical values and practices. As a result, genuine differences over how rights are to be contextualized can and do arise. When they do, the issue must be solved in a way by which legitimate differences between the parties are respected: accommodation is needed. The classical liberal distinction between individuals as pure rational choosers and their membership in various communities is thus much more ambiguous than Trudeau's approach to the Charter suggests.

The Supreme Court of Canada seems to have reached the same conclusion. In *R. v. Oakes*, for example, the Court set out a list of "values and principles," any one of which it thought might provide grounds for a reasonable limitation on a right. This list, intended to "name but a few" of these values and principles, includes, among others, respect for the inherent dignity of the human person, commitment to social justice and equality, accommodation of a wide variety of beliefs and *respect for cultural and group identity*.[7]

One problem the Court fails to solve, however, is how exactly one decides when cultural and group identity ought to be regarded as interests the protection of which reasonably justifies limiting basic freedoms.[8] The Court's growing awareness of the need to make such accommodations, and its concern over the lack of any adequate set of rules or techniques for doing so, has been described by former Supreme Court Justice Bertha Wilson. After reflecting on the difficulties of Charter interpretation and the conceptual problems posed by section 1 of the Charter, she makes the following remarks:

> I do not believe that counsel have yet realized the importance of taking a broader approach to Charter litigation although I think that the Court's recent emphasis on the contextual approach must have brought home to them the need to inform themselves thoroughly on the social context in which the issue arises and that they must appreciate it not only intellectually but emotionally as well. We are in the business now of weighing competing values and values have an emotional and spiritual as well as an intellectual content. So counsel must educate themselves on what it is about a free and democratic society that is so precious. What are its essential elements? When should the rights of the individual or the minority be sacrificed for what the government, i.e., the majority, perceives to be the common good? Or when is this a dangerous path to go down? These are not easy questions to answer and the Court needs all the help it can get...[9]

To say that basic rights are universal thus does not commit one to saying that they must always be applied the same way to all citizens. The logic of a basic right is shaped in part by the social, cultural and political values of the community. In a large, modern, multinational, liberal-democratic, federal state like Canada, sub-groups sometimes have fundamental differences over the nature of their commitment to liberalism.[10] In such circumstances, trying to establish one particular approach to the interpretation of rights through a project of nation building runs the risk of appearing as – and perhaps even of being – a kind of imperialism. Far from uniting the community, this only serves to alienate important subgroups within it.

SOCIAL EQUALITY *VS.* PROVINCIAL AUTONOMY

Pierre Trudeau's pan-Canadian approach to nation building has also been criticized for its effects on social and economic policy. The criticisms focus largely on the claim that key federal powers – such as the spending, taxation, and trade and commerce powers, as well as others falling under the peace, order and good government clause (POGG) – were used by his government to intrude into areas of provincial jurisdiction. Before assessing this claim, let us note two points. First, most of the use of the spending power – which, from the point of view of equality of opportunity, is among the most important of federal powers – has been for shared-cost social programs and equalization. Second, the social and income security programs from old age security through family allowance and medicare were almost entirely mounted by governments from 1950 to the mid-1960s. The use of the federal spending power to make this possible was therefore not an intervention by Trudeau. Only medicare was made law after he became Prime Minister.

Nevertheless, there remains a serious question as to how free the federal government should be to use its spending, taxation and regulatory powers to promote national equality. Certainly some such right exists. Section 36(1)(a) of the Constitution Act, 1982 is the standing demonstration of this. It commits governments to "promoting equal opportunity for the well-being of Canadians." But does the commitment behind this clause justify the free use of key federal powers to promote equality?

Suppose Canada were a unitary state. Further suppose that there were general agreement on the criteria underlying programs aimed at promoting equality of opportunity. Would the scope of the national government's right to use its powers to promote this equality be any greater in this hypothetical unitary Canada than in the existing federal Canada? In short, does the commitment to federalism introduce a norm that in any way alters or limits the pan-Canadian commitment to equality?

In answering this question, let us consider the National Energy Program (NEP) of 1980. It infuriated the West, especially Alberta. Trudeau's attempt to justify the program on the ground that it promoted "equality for all Canadians" did nothing to reduce the outrage. But were the anger and resentment really justified? The answer depends, in part, on how one views federalism. If we assess the NEP in terms of pan-Canadianism, much of the anger seems unwarranted. Once we accept that the commitment to respect regional diversity should be subordinated to the higher good of promoting equality of opportunity, free use of federal powers to redistribute an unexpected increase – a "windfall" – in the wealth and opportunities in one part of the community will look just. And, indeed, many supported the NEP for precisely this reason. If, on the other hand, we accept that the commitment to diversity is to be weighed against individual equality and freedom, Westerners' anger will look justified: the NEP will appear as an excessive use of federal powers – a tax grab – at Westerners' expense. In other words, it will amount to what we called discriminatory redistribution in chapter 2.

We do not want to rehash here the merits and demerits of the NEP. Nevertheless, Westerners' reaction to it drives home the point that attempting to mount a program of nation building through an unqualified use of the federal government's spending, tax and regulatory powers runs a high risk of clashing with deeply felt aspects of regional status and diversity. In our view, Westerners' anger over the NEP reflected their firm conviction that the commitment to federalism implies a respect for regional diversity that imposes limits on the federal government's right to use its powers to promote equality of opportunity. In the absence of such a commitment, this right would be limited only by the moral logic of the equality principle.

Some might shrug here, reply that this is now ancient history and ask whether it really matters. For the foreseeable future, they might say, the prevailing climate of fiscal scarcity is a sufficient guarantee that aggressive use of key federal powers to launch a similar program of nation building is highly unlikely. We are less confident.

Over the next decade, a combination of fiscal scarcity and increasing cross-border economic integration will reshape the federation. Sadly, but realistically, one result may be a substantial increase in regional inequality. On the one hand, fiscal scarcity means the "have-not" provinces, especially in Atlantic Canada, may be facing significant reductions in their present levels of federal support. On the other hand, transnational economic integration could mean that some of the "have" provinces, particularly Alberta and British Columbia, will find themselves entering a whole new growth cycle. If so, the result may be regional disparities that place great pressure on the federal government to aggressively use its powers to redistribute wealth.

As the NEP experience demonstrates, there are limits to what Canadians in "have" provinces will accept as an appropriate effort by the federal government to promote national equality. A first indication of the kinds of tensions this can generate came in the reactions of the three "have" provinces to federally imposed cuts to their share of transfer payments under the Canada Assistance Program. Ontario, in particular, has served notice that it will not tolerate further "unfair" treatment in the distribution of federal money.

Failing to respect what many in "have" provinces see as the fair and just limits imposed on them by federalism thus risks pitting the "haves" against the "have nots." This could divide the country along one of its most volatile faultlines. If Albertans and British Columbians judged that the federal government were placing an unjust burden on their region, trenching on provincial autonomy in the process, they would begin to take steps to isolate themselves – psychologically, economically and politically – from the rest of Canada.

But let us be perfectly clear here. It is precisely because *we support the promotion of national equality* that we think a new meta-vision of Canada must clearly recognize that the federal principle imposes its own limits on the pan-Canadian commitment to promote equality. Our reason is very simple. In order to preserve the legitimacy of the federal government's role as the agent of interprovincial equity in what may prove to be very difficult times ahead, we think it important that the terms and conditions of Canadians' commitment to the sharing community be made more explicit. Our hope is that this will reduce tensions by helping to clarify roles and responsibilities, thus permitting the federal government to act as effectively as possible in its role as the agent of interprovincial equity.

There is a further reason why we think it important that Canadians' commitment to respect regional diversity be both made explicit and systematically explored: it not only must be balanced against the commitment to promote equality of opportunity, but also against the commitment to promote economic efficiency.

Some relatively recent decisions by the Supreme Court suggest that it views new pressures for the harmonization of standards and regulations at the international level – e.g., for controlling pollutants or the general regulation of trade and commerce – as grounds to expand the scope of federal power in ways that trench on provincial jurisdiction. In particular, the Court has appealed to the existence of a "general regulatory" aspect of the trade and commerce power and to a "national dimensions" branch of POGG.[11] Now if, as seems likely, globalization greatly increases pressure for the harmonization of standards and regulations at the international level, this could lead to calls for a rapid and considerable expansion of the scope of these powers. Should the courts go too far too fast in this direction, they could upset the federal-provincial balance.

Thus, globalization seems to be creating tensions not only between provincial autonomy and the promotion of equality of opportunity but also between provincial autonomy and the efficiency goals underlying the economic union.[12] If, as international economic interdependence grows, an adequate federal-provincial balance is to be maintained, the courts, like governments, need a meta-vision that offers some guidance on how to integrate these three fundamental political and juridical norms of Canadian federalism: economic efficiency, national equity and provincial autonomy.

CONCLUSION

Over the last quarter century Canadians have struggled with the task of integrating liberalism and federalism. The remarkable impact that Pierre Trudeau's pan-Canadian vision has had on Canadian political culture is probably best explained by its ability to address the problem in a comprehensive and plausible way. By subordinating diversity to freedom and equality Trudeau was able to champion a nation-building strategy based on universal values such as equality, social justice and individual freedom. Pan-Canadianism thus presents us with the archetypal image of a nation based upon a shared commitment to universal principles of justice: the "just society."

This is the liberal dream of a cosmopolitan society, one in which the common good is defined not by the accidents of history, tradition or custom, but by universal reason. It is an inspiring dream. But do such universal principles of reason, as incorporated in the pan-Canadian vision, really provide an adequate foundation for Canadian federalism? Or must a richer recognition of the unique sociological, historical and cultural features of its communities be built into its basic institutions and laws?

The proof, it seems, is in the pudding. Many Quebecers, Aboriginal peoples and Westerners have all reacted against aspects of the nation-building project by *strengthening* rather than abandoning their attachment to key aspects of their respective political cultures. They have dug in their heels and steadfastly refused to accept that what they regard as essentially community affairs must be subordinated to the new pan-Canadian vision of their common interests. Evidently, they have concluded that this vision imperils certain interests that they take to be vital to their well-being.[13]

The lesson, then, is clear: the original federalist commitment to diversity must be more adequately integrated into the conceptual framework – the meta-vision – that arches over Canadian federalism.

Notes

1. Pierre Elliott Trudeau, "The Values of a Just Society," in Thomas S. Axworthy and Pierre Elliott Trudeau (eds.), *Towards a Just Society* (Markham: Viking, 1990), p. 403, n. 7.

2. Trudeau, "The Values of a Just Society," p. 358.

3. Trudeau, "The Values of a Just Society," pp. 363-64.

4. Trudeau, "The Values of a Just Society," pp. 363-64.

5. Charles Taylor, *Sources of the Self* (Cambridge, Mass.: Harvard University Press, 1989), p. 36. For another attempt to work out such a view, see Bernard Williams, *Ethics and the Limits of Philosophy* (Cambridge, Mass.: Harvard University Press, 1985). For a different and more "individualistic" attempt to integrate community membership into liberal theory, see Will Kymlicka, *Liberalism, Community and Culture* (Oxford: Clarendon Press, 1989).

6. Northrop Frye, *The Great Code: The Bible and Literature* (Toronto: Academic Press Canada, 1982), pp. 86-87.

7. *R. v. Oakes* [1986] 2 S.C.R. 103, in Peter Russell, Rainer Knopff and Ted Morton (eds.), *Federalism and the Charter: Leading Constitutional Decisions* (Ottawa: Carleton University Press, 1989), pp. 456-67 (emphasis added).

8. The Court attempted to solve this problem with the creation of the "*Oakes* test." However, questions have been raised about the adequacy of the test. See Andrew Lokan, "The Rise and Fall of Doctrine Under Section 1 of the Charter," *Ottawa Law Review*, Vol. 24, no. 1 (1992), pp. 163-93.

9. Bertha Wilson "Constitutional Advocacy," *Ottawa Law Review*, Vol. 24, no. 1 (1992), p. 273.

10. Charles Taylor has advanced a similar view of the Canadian political culture. He argues that it contains what he calls deep diversity, that is, at least two fundamentally different visions of the relationship between citizen and state. The result is two different conceptions of liberalism: "procedural liberalism," which is embraced by English-speaking Canada; and "substantive liberalism," which is embraced by many in Quebec. See Charles Taylor, "Can Canada Survive the Charter?", *Alberta Law Review*, Vol. 30, no. 2 (1992), pp. 427-47; and "Shared and Divergent Values," in Ronald L. Watts and Douglas M. Brown (eds.), *Options for a New Canada* (Toronto: University of Toronto Press, 1992), pp. 53-76.

11. On the use of the national concerns doctrine, see *R. v. Crown Zellerbach* [1988] 1 S.C.R. 401; on the use of the general trade power, see *General Motors of Canada v. City National Leasing* [1989] 1, S.C.R. 641. Interesting discussions of these problems can be found in Katherine Swinton, "Federalism Under Fire: The Role of the Supreme Court of Canada," *Law and Contemporary Problems*, Vol. 55, no. 1 (Winter 1992), pp. 121-45; and Robert Howse, "The Labour Conventions Doctrine in an Era of Global Interdependence: Rethinking the Constitutional Dimensions of Canada's External Economic Relations," *Canadian Business Law Journal*, Vol. 16, no. 6 (1990), pp. 160-84.

12. In fact, some provinces have already expressed great concern over this. In particular, Ontario (under David Peterson's Liberal government) threatened to take the federal government to court over provisions in the Canada-US Free Trade Agreement, which affected wine pricing in that province. More recently, Ontario (under Bob Rae's New Democratic Party government) has threatened to challenge federal authority with respect to certain sections of the North American Free Trade Agreement.

13. In a series of six articles published between April 30 and May 6, 1993 in *Le Devoir*, André Burelle examines Pierre Trudeau's philosophical vision of Canada. Our analysis in this chapter parallels Burelle's in a number of respects.

RETHINKING
THE BASIS OF
CANADIAN POLITICAL
COMMUNITY

5

NATION, STATE
AND
POLITICAL COMMUNITY

TWO FORMS OF COMMUNITY, TWO VIEWS OF THE NATION

The state is the set of institutions through which, as the German sociologist Max Weber put it, a monopoly on legitimate coercion is maintained and exercised for a political community to operate. This "monopoly" is territorially defined. The legitimate right of states to exercise power within that territory is their *sovereignty*. Many have viewed the ideal state as one comprised entirely of people of a common language and culture. This is the classical view of the "nation-state." Sweden and Japan are examples of relatively homogeneous nation-states; Canada is not.[1]

State sovereignty in a country like Canada may come into conflict with the principle of *national self-determination*. The idea here is that a group of people with its own history, language and culture constitutes a special kind of community: a "nation." What is special about nations is that their members are united by a relatively well defined set of traditions and interests. According to section 1 of the United Nations International Covenant on Economic, Social and Cultural Rights, a nation that seeks to promote its shared interests has a right to do so. But how is this "right" to be exercised?

In Canadian politics the concept of "the nation" has been used and understood in two quite different ways. On the one hand, nationalists in Quebec and Aboriginal peoples use it in the way described above, that is, as a sociological category that refers to a group with a common linguistic and cultural heritage. On the other hand, liberals such as Pierre Trudeau view it as a political category referring to the citizenry of a single state.[2] "A nation," he wrote in 1968, "is no more and no less than the entire population of a sovereign state."[3] When the word "nation" is used in this way, it is meant to contrast with what we will call "liberal community," with the community that flows from national identity. What is liberal community?

According to liberal theorists, the liberal state is, ideally, an association of free and equal individuals. Liberal politics and society rest on a commitment to respect universal needs and the capacities of persons through the creation of a regime of basic rights. Liberals see any attempt to use state power to force individuals to conform to religiously, culturally or racially defined practices as an abuse of power. The recognition of individual rights is precisely an attempt to rid politics of the inequalities and special privileges so often associated with political systems based on culture and tradition.

For the liberal, then, the sense of solidarity that binds the citizens of a state together is rooted in a common vision of the public, as opposed to the private, life. Liberal community is a result of the mutual respect that citizens feel for one another because of their shared commitment to a politics based on universal principles of freedom, equality and justice. While left- and right-wing liberals may differ over the actual policies implied by these principles, they agree that liberal politics, institutions and practices must be based upon them.

By contrast, nationalists emphasize the importance that individuals attach to their personal identification with a cultural or linguistic group. According to them, this shared identity creates the real bonds that hold a community together. It is what gives members a sense of common purpose. Insofar as this is true, members will naturally feel a desire to protect their collective identity from social, political or economic forces that might erode it. This sense of the overlapping of private and public intensifies when the community feels its existence is threatened, say, by assimilation. In such circumstances, the whole point of having a state may begin to seem inseparable from the idea of protecting the sociological nation. For many community members, the nation-state can begin to appear as the ideal toward which political organization should strive.

So the difference between liberals and nationalists over the basis of political community can be summed up in two key points. First, while liberals think the commitment to a politics based on universal (i.e., impersonal) principles provides an adequate foundation on which to build a stable political culture, nationalists hold that political cohesion and stability also require a shared cultural or linguistic identity. Second, while liberals argue that the state can (and should) remain neutral with respect to the promotion of one such identity over another, nationalists regard the idea that the pursuit of special cultural or linguistic goals can and should be confined to civil society as fallacious and often threatening to a value they consider fundamental.

Is There Middle Ground?

Is a shared cultural or linguistic identity crucial to political community? This is not a frivolous question. For once we have separated the concepts of "nation" and "state," we cannot but realize how far a country like Canada is from being a genuine nation-state. And, indeed, *indépendantistes* in Quebec have pointed to the sociological cleavages in Canadian society and expressed deep doubts about whether an attempt to arrive at a consensus on, say, a substantive legislative agenda aimed at promoting the "common" interest could end in anything other than failure or coercion of some subgroup. In particular, they have argued that the promotion of interests crucial to "English Canada" conflict with those of Quebec. On what basis does Canada rest, then, if not national identity? What is the glue that holds the federation together? Is it purely and simply a liberal community? And, if so, is that really enough?

In our view, a shared commitment to liberal principles is not an adequate foundation on which to build a stable political culture. When one asks why a *particular* liberal state, such as Canada, exists, it is not enough to say that it exists to promote justice, democracy and the freedom and equality of its citizens, and then to explain these in terms of a list of universal human rights. If that is the main justification for Canada's existence, it is a disturbingly weak one; and it becomes hard to see why Canadians should continue to resist the pull of integration with the US. There is, after all, nothing distinctively *Canadian* about the "objectives" of promoting democracy, freedom and equality. Both the American Bill of Rights and the United Nations Declaration of Human Rights contain such a list.

There has long been a gap between what liberals say and what they do on this issue, between their theory and their practice. If, as theorists, they have argued vigorously that liberal states, constitutions and political institutions should be based on universal principles, in practice they have often recognized and accommodated historical interests. In fact, the constitutions and institutions of liberal states everywhere contain all sorts of special obligations, duties, rights and responsibilities, the clear function of which is to protect certain linguistic, cultural and regional communities, as well as various groups and classes. While such provisions often conform to liberal principles,[4] they also often stand in tension with a strict interpretation of liberal principles.[5]

The lesson here is that nationalists are right to insist that liberal states do not rest on a simple collective declaration or act of consent. A group of individuals can no more simply dissolve, by *fiat*, its collective past and establish, by *fiat*, a completely new political order than can an individual dissolve, at will, his or her past and establish, at will, a completely new personality. There is always an historical context surrounding the creation of a new political community and which, more or less implicitly, provides the rationale for its constitution, its political institutions and its existence. Every liberal community, like every person, has its own history, the narrative of which will be interwoven with its understanding of the present and its vision for the future.

If we are right, there is an incompleteness to the claim that liberal polities exist to promote democracy, freedom, equality and liberal justice. In fact, a given liberal state may exist to promote a wide range of objectives, including the sharing of natural wealth and resources, a more efficient promotion of economic interests, peace and military security, increased international prestige and influence, the maintenance of certain cultural practices and the development and enjoyment of a (or some) particular language(s). The commitment to promote freedom and equality has no special connection with any of these and, indeed, sometimes stands in tension with them.

In contrast to liberal values, these "national objectives" reflect certain quite particular, and often unique, interests which the citizens of a given state, or certain subgroups within it, share with one another. But this does not make them secondary concerns. On the contrary, citizens often regard the promotion of these objectives as having the highest priority and as a *prima facie* justification for the exercise of the state's power and the existence of many of its laws and policies. In practice, this means that some claims, goals and objectives have a kind of *de facto* legitimacy or claim on the state's attention that others lack.

In short, the state is not, and should not pretend to be, concerned only that the objectives and goals it promotes conform to liberal principles. On the contrary, the legitimacy of any given liberal state is linked in the minds of its citizens to the promotion of certain quite specific interests and objectives. Some of these will be held in common by all (or most) of the citizens; others will be held only by the members of certain subgroups. To ignore the importance of the latter by treating all liberally acceptable objectives as on a par is to risk alienating those who have legitimate expectations that the state will promote their special interests and who count on it to do so. In the Canadian context, one thinks, for example, of Aboriginal peoples and official language minorities.

Does this mean liberalism must be rejected? The answer is unequivocally no. If we maintain that historical practices and commitments can be regarded as a legitimate source of expectations, claims, rights or obligations – some of which may impinge on individual freedom or equality – it certainly does *not* follow that any collection of individuals with a shared identity can expect the state to protect or promote that identity. While federalism represents a commitment to diversity, this commitment is not open-ended. In Canada, it is aimed at accommodating certain quite specific forms of linguistic, cultural and regional diversity that are central to Canadians' shared history. But which specific policies can federalism be invoked to justify?

Here the concept of the meta-vision is relevant. An adequate meta-vision for Canadian federalism would involve an understanding of, and commitment to respect, the basic forms of diversity, along with some indication of how these are to be weighed against liberal rights when the two conflict. In a nutshell, a meta-vision must do justice to the liberal aim of founding politics on universal principles, without ignoring Canadians' shared history.

These issues will be discussed further in the next chapter. Our main point here is that liberals, in their theory, rhetoric and polemics, have tended to exaggerate the role that universal principles play in establishing and maintaining political community, while understating the importance of historical ties. To hear some liberals speak, one is left with the impression that, in a "truly" liberal society, the idea that the state might show a preference for the interests of certain communities over others should be shunned – the doctrine of neutrality. Yet, as Pierre Trudeau – perhaps the most influential exponent of this view – once remarked, maintaining political cohesion in modern states requires that a special kind of "consensus" be reached among different interests in the community. Such a consensus, he tells us, "is a mysterious process which takes in many elements, such as language, communications, associations, geographical proximity, tribal origins, common interests and history, external pressures and even foreign intervention..."[6]

We take this to mean that, if modern liberal states like Canada are to remain united, they must show respect for, and a sensitivity to, the unique mission that their own histories have placed upon them. If so, the urgent task that liberals in Canada now face is one of integrating more satisfactorily the recognition of universal principles with the respect for our shared history – that is, of a regionally diverse country, founded by two peoples of different language and culture and now attempting to incorporate Aboriginal peoples on a basis of full recognition. In the Canadian context, this means in effect that two things about liberal equality be accepted: *first, that it is not inconsistent with the recognition of official forms of diversity in the Constitution; and, second, that it does not require that the entitlements, rights and responsibilities that would flow from such a recognition be distributed identically among citizens or governments.* Only in coming to terms with these two points will the liberal tradition in Canada be able to reconcile itself with the federalist one.

From Nation-State to Political Community

We agree with the nationalists that political community requires more than just a commitment to liberal freedom and equality. Nevertheless, we remain liberals. For, unlike nationalists, we think the task of securing community presupposes neither that there must already be, nor that the state must seek to create, a single over-arching national identity. Indeed, in large multinational states such as Canada, the attempt to forge such an identity is likely only to pit one nationalism against another.

The endless search for, the vague allusions to and the desire to create "the Canadian identity" only make sense against a backdrop of assumptions that treat the country as a (relatively) closed system which, ideally, would be bounded by a "nation" in the sociological sense. In short, once the liberal rhetoric is stripped away, one often finds an underlying allegiance to the classical theory of the nation-state. Certainly, this is how many viewed the nation-building exercise of the early 1980s.[7] The results of that initiative have convinced us that fighting nationalism with nationalism is a formula for division, not unity.

The alternative is to revise the idea of liberal pluralism to include a respect for communities as well as individuals. This amounts to accepting that countries such as Canada are and should remain sociologically diverse; and that, as a result, individual citizens often have multiple allegiances. In such a state, "nation building" will still aim to promote political cohesion, integration and stability. But it will do so from within the framework of a pluralistic meta-vision, not by developing a single national identity. Perhaps, then, we should speak instead of "community building." Such a community-building program would be derived from four sources:

- a shared commitment to liberal principles;
- a respect for Canadians' shared history, including a respect for those particular values, objectives and purposes that led to the founding of the country;
- a respect for the particular forms of sociological diversity that run through that history, with specific consideration for the Aboriginal "diversity" neglected in 1867; and
- a vision for the future, that is, an agenda that promotes the over-arching values and objectives toward which the community as a whole is working.

On this approach, federal and provincial governments may sometimes have a special obligation to promote the interests associated with a particular cultural, linguistic or regional identity. However, the proposed pluralism – what we call *federal pluralism* – would assume that no single identity embraces the whole range of a citizen's interests, the way national identities traditionally have been thought to do. To say that one is a Dene or *Québécois* would thus be a way of identifying important interests an individual has; but the same person will have other interests – economic, social and cultural – that are relatively unconnected to membership in one of these "national" communities. Federal pluralism is essentially a response to the fact that identities are increasingly complex.

As a result of globalization, multiple allegiances are no longer limited to the forms of diversity *within* the federation. Citizens are developing new associations, attachments, commitments and loyalties *beyond* Canada's borders. New "transnational" allegiances are forming based on, for example, membership in human rights organizations or the environmental movement.[8] Already, this is creating tensions between different levels of interest, such as the conflict between the Canadian forestry industry and the international environmental movement.[9]

As globalization progresses, it will further fragment citizens' allegiances. This, in turn, may diminish the importance of national identities. This does not mean that the identities of, say, *Québécois* or First Peoples will cease to exist or to play an important role in politics and private life. Rather, individual members of those "national" communities are becoming aware that they have politically relevant interests that, increasingly, they associate with neither a particular state nor "nation." This will make the old ideal of the nation-state – that is, a self-contained, territorially defined entity whose citizens are united by a single, over-arching identity – look increasingly anachronistic.

Thus, while hitherto we have spoken informally of Canada as a "political community," we now wish to invest that term with a more specific meaning. From now on we use it to mark a shift in the tone and emphasis of our analysis as we attempt to move away from the traditional way of thinking and talking about Canada as a nation-state and toward a conception of it as a liberal political community.

Notes

1. As we saw in the last chapter, however, the tradition of nation building has been a part of Canada's history. In that tradition, the idea of the nation-state is broader and includes those states that use their power to foster a sense of national identity. Some of the central concepts and arguments in this tradition will be further discussed below.

2. Or perhaps the citizenry and the state taken together.

3. Pierre Elliott Trudeau, "Federalism, Nationalism, and Reason," *Federalism and the French Canadians* (Toronto: Macmillan, 1968), p. 187.

4. For example, the commitment to equality of opportunity in section 36 of the Constitution Act, 1982 seems to flow from liberal views.

5. The language rights in the Canadian Charter are a case in point. Insofar as the Charter is supposed to be a liberal document, we think it not only fails to justify but also quite possibly conflicts with their entrenchment. Nevertheless, when one considers the historical role of the French and English languages in Canada, and the crucial role they continue to play in fostering a sense of community, the entrenchment of these rights is eminently defensible. This will be discussed in the next chapter.

6. Trudeau, "Federalism, Nationalism, and Reason," p. 189.

7. In "Federalism, Nationalism, and Reason," written in 1964, Pierre Trudeau speculated about the possibility of using nationalism at the federal level to counter a rise in nationalism at the provincial level (pp. 182-203). Many have seen the nation-building project of the early 1980s as an attempt to put these ideas into effect. See, for example, Robert Comeau, "Entrevue avec Robert Comeau," in Gilles Gougeon (ed.), *Histoire du nationalisme Québécois : Entrevues avec sept spécialistes* (Montréal: vlb éditeur, 1994), p. 150; Alain-G. Gagnon and Guy Laforest, "The future of federalism: lessons from Canada and Quebec," *International Journal*, Vol. 48, no. 3 (Summer 1993), pp. 470-91.

8. See, for example, Michael Walzer, "The new political ideologies," *The Economist*, September 11-17, 1993, pp. 49-52 in the insert "The Future Surveyed."

9. See Will Kymlicka and Donald G. Lenihan, "Whither the Nation-State: Finding a Niche in the Global Village," *Policy Options*, Vol. 15, no. 6 (July-August 1994), pp. 11-14.

6

FEDERAL PLURALISM: SOME ARGUMENTS AND DISTINCTIONS

The Collective Rights Issue

In the last chapter the concept of federal pluralism was introduced. We argued that a recognition of "official forms of diversity" is not inconsistent with the commitment to liberalism. In this chapter we anticipate two main objections to federal pluralism.

The first is that, if recognizing certain communities as "official" ones involves the recognition of "community" or "collective" rights, this would violate Canadians' liberal commitment to the primacy of the individual.[1] In this view, the debate over collective or community rights comes down to a single, fundamental question: should a liberal-democratic society recognize the existence of individual *and* collective rights, or just individual ones? Those who take the latter position raise what we call the "theoretical" objection to federal pluralism; they maintain that community rights are inconsistent with the commitment to respect individual equality and freedom.

We agree that there is a theoretical tension between individual and collective rights. Nevertheless, Canada, as a liberal-democratic federal state, is committed to both. A more principled way of balancing the two must be found. The first step is to develop a more sophisticated view of what community rights are, why they are important and how they affect Canadian political debate and state-craft. We explore these issues below.

The second objection is more a practical than a theoretical one. It arises from what we call the "Pandora's box problem." Once the state recognizes one group as an official community with special rights, why should it not recognize others? What stops every other interest group from claiming that it too constitutes a community that merits official recognition and special rights?

Claims now advanced in the name of community or collective rights come from a wide range of sources, including Aboriginal people, language groups, ethnic minorities, the women's movement, the disabled and homosexuals. We agree that, if there is no reasonably principled way to decide which ones can justly claim a community right, say, to some degree of autonomy, constitutional recognition or special representation in national institutions, the attempt to base Canadian politics more clearly on federal pluralism could degenerate into a free-for-all that would undermine the commitment to representative democracy.

However, the Pandora's box problem is not intractable. Many claims advanced as community or collective rights involve concerns over some form of discrimination. Such claims may be important and just. But they are quite different from the concerns over community that underlie federalism. To describe the right to equal treatment as a community right is a category error. This does not mean the grievance is any less pressing or important. But recognizing it does affect the way we assess and respond to such claims. It also makes the Pandora's box problem far less threatening, as we discuss in greater detail later in this chapter.

Two Kinds of Rights?

The theoretical objection to federal pluralism falsely suggests that individual rights make up a single well-defined class. It then approaches collective rights as different sorts of claims that stand in opposition to individual ones and that compete with them. This is misleading in at least two ways.

First, it assumes that the task of balancing individual rights is one of balancing competing aspects of individual liberty and equality, while the task of balancing individual and collective rights is one of deciding how far the interests of the collectivity should be allowed to erode personal freedom – that is, to trump individual rights. Second, it assumes that individual rights are unambiguously individual while collective rights are unambiguously collective.

In fact, the distinction between individual and collective rights is far less clear than most discussions of the issue suggest. There are important cases where the meaningful exercise of what is supposed to be an individual right will not be possible without the existence of a community.[2] When this happens, the claim that the right is individual rather than collective may be controversial or even arbitrary. To put it somewhat differently, some rights have both individual and collective *aspects*.[3]

Exploring this ambiguity in the structure of some rights helps us to see more clearly why collective or community rights are essential to federalism and how they relate to the liberal commitment to respect individual freedom and equality. We will approach the problem through an analysis of the language rights in section 23 of the Charter.

DISTINGUISHING INDIVIDUAL FROM COLLECTIVE RIGHTS

Most scholars agree that the language rights in the Charter are vested in individuals. On this point, the wording is quite clear. But is legal wording the sole criterion for determining when a right is individual or collective?

Suppose we ask why it is that French and English are protected by the Charter. Why not, say, Chinese or Italian? Or why not all four languages? How should a defender of the Charter's language rights reply? The stock answer is that the French and the English were "founding communities" (or perhaps "founding peoples") while the Chinese and Italians were not.

In this view, the historical place of these "linguistic communities," along with the fact that French and English have been, *de facto,* the languages of Canada for more than 250 years, justifies the current status of those languages as official ones. The early history and founding of Canada is viewed as a collaborative effort that involved a series of important political arrangements between the French-speaking *Canadiens* and the British. As a result, those living today who are members of these original language communities have a claim on the country regarding the choice of its official languages that the Chinese and Italian communities lack. On this view, the historical role of the *Canadiens* and British gave them a "right" to have their own languages recognized as the official ones of the country. But two questions need to be posed here.

First, if there is a justification in history and long practice for these language rights, who is the bearer of the rights? Is it the French- and English-speaking *communities?* Or is it the *members* of these communities? In short, is the right a collective or an individual one? Second, what sort of "rights" are we actually talking about?

The Language Rights in the Charter: A Closer Look

Consider the right to freedom of conscience. This is a relatively uncontroversial example of an individual human right. It is supposed to protect a particular capacity of individuals, the free exercise of which is thought crucial to their full development as human beings. In this case, it is their capacity to freely choose a religion (or to withhold belief). To say that the capacity is an "individual" one is to say that *it can be both held and exercised by individuals,* acting alone. The traditional liberal civil and democratic rights, taken together, are supposed to provide the minimum protection necessary to individuals to allow them to exercise their capacity for free choice and self-development.

But to speak of a "capacity for free choice" is to speak in very general terms. No basis is given to distinguish a Quebecer from an Albertan or either of these from a Saudi or a Nigerian. A right that is supposed to protect something as abstract as a "capacity for choice" will therefore be of universal application – which is why we call rights justified in this way *human* rights. The *language* rights in the Charter differ from individual human rights in at least two ways.

First, a language is not something that can be produced, maintained, exercised or enjoyed by individuals acting alone. Language is by its very nature a collective enterprise. Its existence presupposes the existence of a community of users. The community provides the setting in which the development, use and maintenance of a language takes place. Language, as a social activity, is unthinkable without others to talk to.

In practical terms, this makes the preservation and vitality of a language community a condition for the exercise of language rights, in a way that the preservation and vitality of a community of believers is not a condition for the exercise of free choice regarding religious beliefs. If so, these language rights are not individual ones in the same sense as freedom of conscience.

Second, the language rights in the Charter cannot be intended solely to protect a bare "human capacity" (e.g., for speech). If they were, all who had this capacity – i.e., all who could speak – would have an equal right to have their own language constitutionally protected. But the Charter specifically singles out English and French. The language rights in the Charter therefore cannot be justified in the same way as human rights.[4] The legal wording notwithstanding, they are neither universal nor fully individual. They are *particular* and partly *collective.*

They are particular in the sense that, if they can be justified, it will not be by reference to a general human capacity that the rights are supposed to protect. It will be on largely *historical* grounds; that is, it will have to be shown that these rights have been *justly acquired* and given the sanction of long and uncontested usage. The rights are collective in the sense that they cannot be exercised and enjoyed by individuals, acting alone. They have a crucial collective aspect.

The historical and collectivist character of these rights is most evident in the case of the minority language education rights in section 23 of the Charter. Thus, in the *Mahé* judgement, then Chief Justice Brian Dickson wrote:

A notion of equality between Canada's official language groups is obviously present in section 23. Beyond this, however, the section is, if anything, an exception to the provisions of sections 15 and 27 [which guarantee individual equality and respect for the "multicultural heritage" of Canadians, respectively] in that it accords these groups, the French and the English, special status in comparison to all other linguistic groups in Canada...[I]t would be totally incongruous to invoke in aid of the interpretation of a provision which grants special rights to a select group of individuals, the principle of equality intended to be universally applicable to "every individual."[5]

The legal wording vests section 23 rights in individuals; nevertheless, before individuals can claim them they must meet certain criteria. These criteria are different from such usual rights-conferring considerations as need, the protection of human powers, compensation for some disadvantage or personal merit. On the contrary, the rights are granted on the basis of what, on first blush, appears to be a rather arbitrary characteristic: the fact that the individual belongs to a particular linguistic community. Such membership is usually an accident of birth.

If these rights belonged strictly to individuals, the only explanation for their apparently arbitrary distribution would be that they were a kind of "institutional inheritance," much like an aristocratic title. Some people would be fortunate enough to receive them, others would not. As we will see, there is a grain of truth in this analysis. Nevertheless, as it stands, it is a very unsatisfactory – even alarming – defence of the language rights in section 23. Could it really be fair that some people are singled out by the state for preferential treatment, simply because their ancestors arrived in the country a little earlier than those of some others?

The seeming arbitrariness here results from trying to understand these rights as though they stood in the same relationship to individuals as human rights. If we look on them as a mechanism to protect individual choice, it is difficult to see why some citizens' capacity for choice is more important than that of others. But this obscures the fact that these rights also have a collective social function: they are *instruments of community integration and political cohesion.* As such, they are grounded in the original commitment to federalism. They are an expression of the fact that linguistic duality is a fundamental characteristic of Canada's historical diversity. The respect for that diversity is a defining feature of Canada as a political community.

This view of the origin and role of the rights affects their logic in two very important ways. First, it reveals that they are more than a way of protecting individual choice. They are also a kind of political institution for maintaining the integrity and the unique character of some important aspect of Canadian society, namely, linguistic duality. As a result, they no longer look like an arbitrary *individual* inheritance but rather as a means for preserving and promoting a central element in Canadians' *collective* sense of community. As such, they belong to the community *as a whole.*

Second, this viewpoint helps us understand why singling out French and English for special treatment is not a form of discrimination against those with another first language. Immigrants usually come to their new country *as individuals* who, on choosing to become citizens, are assumed to have accepted the fundamental character of the Canadian community they are seeking to join.[6] In the Canadian case, this includes a respect for the commitment to linguistic dualism and for the measures (legitimately) agreed upon for preserving it.

This does *not* mean governments have no responsibility for helping immigrants adjust to their new society; nor does it mean that immigrants can make no legitimate claims with respect to their own cultural and linguistic needs. It simply means that the responsibilities of governments, and the legitimacy of such claims, are based upon and limited by other considerations and commitments.[7]

If this argument is right, those who use what we called the theoretical argument to oppose the entrenchment of any collective rights, yet who defend bilingualism, would seem to be inconsistent. Their support for bilingualism amounts to an implicit recognition and acceptance of the importance of some kinds of collective interests as well as of some version of the pact theory.[8] If those who presently insist that any recognition of collective rights infringes on individual liberty continue to insist on the validity of this argument, then, in our view, they should bite the bullet and draw the further conclusion that there is no liberal way to justify *any* special language rights. A consistent classical liberal individualist will therefore hold that no individual's language should be singled out for special treatment. The interests of *each and every citizen* should be treated equally by the state.[9] For our part, we regard this conclusion as a *reductio ad absurdum* of the theoretical argument against collective rights.

LEGAL RIGHTS *VS.* INDIVIDUAL AND COLLECTIVE INTERESTS

Our discussion of rights has moved freely back and forth between talk of *legal* rights – that is, those specified by law – and the (individual or collective) *interests* that someone might point to in order to justify the introduction of laws that protect these rights. For example, insofar as Canadians agree that their freedom of expression should be guaranteed in the Charter, it is presumably because they believe that their well-being is importantly linked to this freedom – so much so, that their interest in free expression merits protection under the law.[10]

When people talk in this context of their right to freedom of expression, they are not speaking of their *legal* right – that is, a right prescribed by law; no such right may exist. They are talking about their "human" or "moral" rights. Which interests merit such protection is, of course, a matter for debate. Nevertheless, respect for the basic democratic and civil rights is now internationally recognized as part of the core of any adequate account of human dignity and freedom. The great moral power behind these rights derives precisely from the fact that the interests underlying them are universal and capable of being rendered individual.

By contrast, we contended that the interests underlying the language rights in the Charter are particular and partly collective. The justification for giving priority to one language over another involves historical considerations about its place and use in the community. From these considerations we derive two criteria by which a collective interest can be distinguished from an individual one:

- when the protection and promotion of the interest is linked to some special kind of community activity;

- when a description of the interest involves some account of a community's unique historical experience.

Federalism was a response to just such concerns. Originally, it was intended to accommodate the special interests of two kinds of communities: the regional ones; and the two linguistic groups. Aboriginal peoples have since protested their relative exclusion from the original project. Identifying the provinces and territories as the regional communities, we will call these three communities "federal" ones. They are federal in the sense that, as communities, they have a special significance in the Canadian political community that stems from the commitment to found the country on a respect for diversity through federalism.

The special interests of these communities are protected through a variety of measures associated with the federal tradition. Two obvious ones are the creation of provincial legislatures and the establishment of the Senate as a regionally representative institution. The Constitution Act, 1867 entrenched measures reflecting the country's commitment to linguistic duality; further measures on language were included in the Charter in 1982. The protection of Aboriginal rights in section 35 of the Charter was an important step toward greater recognition of Aboriginal peoples' special interests in Confederation. Federal pluralism is based on the thesis that the recognition of these three communities forms part of the fundamental definition of Canada. If this is accepted, it becomes easier to see how the Pandora's box problem can be brought under control.

Collective Legal Rights: Remedial Measures vs. Defining Features

After 1982 the Charter became a springboard for a new class of groups with important political claims: the so-called "equality-seeking" groups. During the debates over the Meech Lake and Charlottetown accords some in this movement began to employ the language of collective rights – i.e., of federalism – to advance the claims of women, the disabled and gays.

At the federally sponsored Conference on Institutional Reform, held in Calgary on January 23-26, 1992, the full political implications of this new direction began to become apparent. Advocates from the western provinces had been arguing for a reformed Senate that would increase regional representation at the centre. Spokespersons for the equality-seeking groups countered with a proposal to transform the

Senate into a "House of Equality" where the collective interests of disadvantaged social groups, such as women and the disabled, would be represented. What are we to make of this attempt by equality-seeking groups to co-opt the historic discourse and an institution of federalism to advance their objectives?

We have argued that special representation or rights for collectivities is not, of itself, either illiberal or anti-democratic. However, for such claims to have legitimacy, it is not enough that a group have important and politically relevant interests to promote. It also needs to be shown that their interests will not be represented fairly by others who do not share them. Can equality-seeking groups establish such a claim?[11]

What are the politically relevant interests at stake for groups such as women, gays and the disabled? The answer is clear: equality. Members of these groups claim to suffer from *discrimination*. Their membership in a certain class results in their not being treated equally with others. This is a serious and important concern. But it is not a collective interest that is at issue. It is an individual one: their right as citizens to be treated equally with others.

Can advocates of equality-seeking groups establish that their interests in equality will not be adequately represented by others? There are two ways to understand this claim.

On the one hand, it could mean that individuals' particular interests in equality can only be fairly represented by someone who shares them (e.g., "only women can speak for women"; "only the disabled can speak for the disabled"; etc.). If this is the basis of the claim for special representation, it must be rejected. To accept it would be to undermine the foundations of representative democracy. Representative democracy rests on the assumption that individual citizens' interests in freedom and equality can be fairly represented by others. If we could not entrust that task to others, we would have to be present to represent ourselves every time decision making occurs, which is simply impossible.

On the other hand, the claim could mean that there are times when members of a particular collection of individuals have good reason to believe that entrusting their interests in equality to others would lead to or reinforce discrimination. Thus, say, the disabled might argue that able-bodied persons genuinely *do not understand the nature of the problems faced by disabled persons and hence cannot be expected to adequately represent their interests.* If it could be convincingly shown that such ignorance existed and imperiled their right to equality, some special rights or representation in decision making might well be justified. But let us note two points.

First, if under such circumstances some sort of special representational rights were granted, it would not be a consequence of the nature of the interest at stake, that is, equality. It would be in response to the existing state of ignorance in the society. Second, if this ignorance were overcome, say, by public education, there would no longer be a justification for maintaining the special rights. The claim, therefore, is based upon a contingent set of circumstances. The special rights would be a *temporary remedial measure* aimed at overcoming the particular obstacle to individual equality.

This is precisely the goal of affirmative action plans. They involve the use of collective wording in legal texts to protect an individual interest in equality. This can be an effective way of eliminating discrimination. But such measures are, by definition, temporary and remedial. This is *not* the case with the language or Aboriginal rights protected in the Charter, or the powers of the legislatures set out in section 92 of the Constitution Act, 1867. These are all *defining features* of the political community. As such they are quasi-permanent.[12]

The different role that the two kinds of collective legal rights play obliges us to distinguish between the various kinds of laws and institutions that give effect to them. Thus, while collectively worded remedial measures may be acceptable at the statute level – statutes being relatively temporary measures – it seems inappropriate to entrench them in the Constitution. The latter is a tool of statecraft intended to shape and define the permanent features of the larger community. By contrast, the Constitution is a reasonable place to articulate those characteristics of federal communities that are defining features of the country. Similarly, one might take a variety of collectively worded remedial measures (affirmative action plans) to improve the representation of certain groups within Parliament, such as women, gays or the disabled. But it makes little sense to define the structure of the Senate, one of the country's central institutions, in terms of the very inequalities that the measures are supposed to overcome.

While we think it is inappropriate for equality-seeking groups to co-opt the political discourse of federalism and of community rights, this does not mean we deny that women, gays or the disabled constitute a community in the sociological sense. It may be that members of these groups share a sense of community based on common interests and concerns. Perhaps one can even speak of a "gay culture" or the "way of life" of the disabled. But this still would not change the fact that the issues they are collectively seeking to address are largely concerned with promoting individual equality and eliminating discrimination. These issues therefore should be presented, debated and addressed in the language of individual rights, not federalism.

THE CITIZEN-STATE RELATION: SOME DISTINCTIONS

Pulling together the main points from the discussion so far, we can construct a framework of four basic ways in which the citizen-state relationship can be conceptualized:[13]

1. It may be agreed that there are collective interests (e.g., a minority language community's right to have its language protected) but that, at the legal level, these rights should be framed in individualist language (i.e., by identifying individuals as the legal bearers of the entitlements).

In our view, this is the best way to understand section 17 of the Charter, which states that: "Everyone has the right to use English or French in any debates or other proceedings of Parliament." The wording clearly assigns the right to individuals. Nevertheless, as we have already argued, the interest that justifies the existence of such a right is, we believe, a collective one.

2. Someone may accept that there are collective interests and then insist that the collective nature of these interests should be reflected in the legal language.

This seems to have been the view of the framers of the British North America Act when in section 93(1) they expressly attributed certain educational rights to any "Class of persons" that fell within conditions that related to the predominant religions at the time of Confederation. The use of collectivist language here makes it clear that the communities have the right, as communities, to manage the institutions in question.

It is worth contrasting section 93(1) with the language rights in section 23 of the Charter. In the latter case, the legal wording assigns the rights to individuals, not collectivities. As a result there was some question as to whether the right extended to the communities involved, thus allowing them to manage the institutions. In *Mahé v. Alberta* the Court agreed that it did. This confirms the collectivist nature of the interest at issue. But the fact that there were genuine doubts that the right had collective implications also underlines the important role legal wording plays in shaping the Court's approach to interpretation.

3. It could be argued that all interests are individual, but that, in some cases, the creation of collective legal rights is appropriate.

As argued above, positive measures to overcome discrimination, such as affirmative action programs, seem to be of this sort.

4. Finally, it could be argued that all moral rights are individual ones and that therefore all legal rights should be individual as well.

This last position provides the base from which to advance what we called the theoretical argument against federal pluralism. It is also the view underlying classical liberalism.

Before concluding, we wish to consider briefly some recent developments in the jurisprudence of the Supreme Court. As it has struggled with the task of interpreting the Charter, it has had to deal with the tensions between the four basic distinctions set out above. Its experience is instructive.

BALANCING COLLECTIVE AND INDIVIDUAL RIGHTS: THE ROLE OF SECTION 1 OF THE CHARTER

Section 1 of the Charter states that Charter rights are "subject only to such reasonable limits prescribed by law as can be demonstrably justified in a free and democratic society." Initially, the Supreme Court interpreted this section narrowly, taking it as an instruction to decide whether an impugned law infringed a protected right. In general, if it did, it would be unconstitutional.[14]

What quickly came to light, however, was that other constitutionally protected values and goals exist – some of which are collective in nature. The Court could not just subordinate them to individual Charter rights, so it was forced to conclude that such values and goals must be balanced against the individual rights in the Charter. In *R. v. Oakes*,[15] four years after the introduction of the Charter, the Supreme Court took a major step by attempting to develop a framework that would allow it to use section 1 as a mechanism to balance individual Charter rights with other competing goals and values.

The *Oakes* test has two branches. The first requires that the Court decide whether the objective of the legislation in question is important enough to justify overriding a right or freedom protected by the Charter. If the legislation passes the test, it then must be examined under the second branch. This is designed to test the adequacy of the relationship between means (i.e., the measures in the legislation) and end (i.e., the objective of the legislation). Our interest here is in the first branch.

As Janet Hiebert notes, by the time of *Oakes* the Court had "recognized that it would have to evaluate the merits of contentious policies to determine whether protected rights should be qualified for general or collective goals of fundamental importance."[16] The first branch of *Oakes* was supposed to yield a fairly rigorous approach to weighing competing objectives and values. However, since *Oakes* the Court has found that part of the test far less rigorous and far more speculative than it had first thought. In part, this reflects the fact that the structure of some Charter rights is far more complex than the legal wording suggests.

While the individualist cast of the wording suggests that all Charter rights focus unambiguously on the protection of individual interests, this, as we have seen, is not always the case. The role of some rights is ambiguous: often they protect individual choice but sometimes they protect the community. Thus in the *Mahé* case, when the Court explored the collective implications of section 23, it found that the rights extended to protect the French-speaking communities' interest in managing their own schools. In such cases, the Court's task goes beyond balancing one individual right against another; it also requires a kind of "internal balancing" of the individual and collective aspects of the right. The clear lesson is that there is often much more to a right than what is suggested by the words in the legal text.

The task of working out the logic underlying the Charter is daunting. There is also a risk that the justices will inject into the jurisprudence their own subjective views about what are the fundamental values and goals of Canadian society. This creates a serious dilemma for the Court. On the one hand, there seems to be no rigorous test to define the balance between competing values and goals. On the other, if the Court is not to lose legitimacy, the justices must have more to go on when reviewing legislation than their own subjective judgements about what is best for the country.[17]

Recognizing the political awkwardness of this situation, the Court has since tended to treat the first branch of the *Oakes* test as almost *pro forma*, allowing most legislation to proceed to the second stage with little scrutiny.[18] But this "answer" to the dilemma cannot be more than a stop-gap. Sooner or later, the Court must come to terms with the problem of balancing competing values and goals.

In fact, a somewhat different approach may already be emerging. In 1989, in *Edmonton Journal v. Alberta,* the Court proposed a somewhat different approach to the problem of balancing, one that lies midway between a formal test and a subjective judgement. It suggested that the rights in the Charter need to be *contextualized.* As Madam Justice Wilson describes it:

> One virtue of the contextual approach...is that it recognizes that a particular right or freedom may have a different value depending on the context...The contextual approach attempts to bring into sharp relief the aspect of the right or freedom which is truly at stake in the case as well as the relevant aspects of any values in competition with it. It seems to be more sensitive to the reality of the dilemma posed by particular facts and therefore more conducive to finding a fair and just compromise between the two competing values under section 1.[19]

The Court's experience with the *Oakes* test seems to have led it to conclude that the goal of developing a single interpretive framework for the Charter is too ambitious. Nevertheless, the contextual approach proposed in *Edmonton Journal* suggests that it may still be possible to develop a series of frameworks or contexts for analyzing certain kinds of tensions in the Charter.[20] We think this is a promising alternative. Indeed, federal pluralism is an attempt to develop such a framework or context for balancing Canadians' twin commitments to federalism and liberalism.

Insofar as the Charter entrenches traditional liberal individual rights, Canada is no different than any other liberal-democratic state, such as the United States, France, Germany or Britain. Liberal rights identify and protect what is universal in individuals – certain "human capacities." But, as we saw in the last chapter, for just this reason the commitment to liberalism cannot be what distinguishes the Canadian political community from other liberal-democratic countries. Liberal rights must rather be viewed as a fundamental *background condition* against which any modern conception of justice and politics should be defined. To say that Canadians are committed to liberalism therefore tells only part of the story of what their political community is about. There remains the crucial question of how liberal rights and values are to be *applied* in that community.

The wording of section 1 does not capture this. Taken at face value, it instructs us to limit rights by asking what is consistent with the abstract *idea* of a free and democratic society. This falsely implies that section 1 arguments should be limited to general or theoretical considerations about the way various universal rights and freedoms interact to restrict one another, or how rights must be restricted to ensure that everybody benefits equally from them.

These are certainly important considerations. But this "theoretical" approach to section 1 ignores the fact that in any actual liberal society rights interact with, limit and are limited by the society's *unique* values, practices, objectives and commitments.[21] From this "particularist" point of view, section 1 no longer appears confined to theoretical questions about free and democratic societies *in general.* It also asks how freedom and democracy are to be understood *in Canada:* what is essential to the *Canadian* vision of liberal democracy?

From this perspective, "reasonable limits" are defined by what is required to respect the special historical needs and aspirations of the community as a whole. And this is just what is at issue when we reflect on the interests underlying the federal components of the Charter, such as the language rights, Aboriginal rights and the recognition of multiculturalism. While it would be too glib to say that, from the point of view of federalism, the way to contextualize the liberal rights in the Charter is to respect Canada's history, it is at least fair to say that those rights cannot be contextualized without a deep appreciation of and respect for that history. Federal pluralism is an attempt to identify the crucial characteristics of Canada as a particular political community in a way that, among other things, helps us to achieve a better balance between the liberal and federal components of the Charter and thereby to work toward the development of a truly Canadian vision of liberalism.

Conclusion

On the classical liberal's assumptions, legislation that infringes individual liberties in order to promote community interests appears as an unjustified "collectivist" assault on individual freedom. In this view, any such legislation ought to be struck down under the first branch of the *Oakes* test. But once we recognize that there are already many cases where Canadians quite legitimately weigh collective against individual interests, the same law may begin to appear as a reasonable attempt to balance various competing values and goals in a way that will promote the overall well-being of both individual citizens and the community.

Passing legislation that identifies and protects rights is one way to protect an interest. And there are many different kinds of interests. Some are individual; some are collective. Some are important enough to merit protection in law; many are not. When legal protection is in order, the best choice of wording will vary with time and place. Sometimes the best strategy will be to use collectivist wording; sometimes individualist wording; sometimes a combination of both. Judgement is called for. All that can be said in advance is that, over the long term, legislators should aim at pre-serving a balance between the promotion of those interests that have a collective aspect and those that are more unambiguously individual.

Notes

1. It is worth noting that, in fact, the Constitution already recognizes the existence of some collective rights. Section 93(1) of the Constitution Act, 1867 limits the powers of the legislature of a province to make laws in respect of education by providing that "[n]othing in any such Law shall prejudicially affect any Right or Privilege with respect to Denominational Schools which any Class of Persons have by Law in the Province at the Union."

It is a "Class of Persons" that has the "Right or Privilege," not the individuals within the Class. If the right is infringed, Section 93(3) provides that "an Appeal shall lie to the Governor General in Council from any Act or Decision of any Provincial Authority affecting any Right or Privilege of the Protestant or Roman Catholic Minority of the Queen's Subjects in relation to Education." The "Class of Persons" or "the Minority" as collectivities must be vested with the rights since they cannot be effectively exercised by individuals except in groups. Judgements of our courts at different times since Confederation have made clear the importance of this collective right.

Section 35 of the Constitution Act, 1982 "recognizes and affirms" the "existing aboriginal and treaty rights of the aboriginal peoples of Canada." It is our view that any adequate attempt to make these rights explicit at the constitutional level would require that they too be treated as the rights of collectivities, namely "the aboriginal peoples."

2. Pierre Carignan, "De la notion de droit collectif et de son application en matière scolaire au Québec," *La revue juridique Thémis*, Vol. 18, no. 1 (1984), pp. 24-37.

3. The idea that the interests underlying rights can have both collective and individual aspects is discussed in Leslie Green, "Two Views of Collective Rights," *The Canadian Journal of Law and Jurisprudence*, Vol. 4, no. 2 (July 1991), pp. 315-29; and in Denise Réaume, "Individuals, Groups, and Rights to Public Goods," *University of Toronto Law Journal*, Vol. 38, no. 1 (1988), pp. 1-27.

4. This is not to say that there are no general claims about the human capacity for language that will ground individual language rights. We think there are. Rather, these considerations do not explain the particular language rights in the Charter. On the connection between equality, language and the Charter, see Gordon Scott Campbell, "Language, Equality and the *Charter*: Collective Versus Individual Rights in Canada and Beyond," *National Journal of Constitutional Law*, Vol. 4, no. 1 (1993), pp. 29-73.

5. See Campbell, "Language, Equality and the *Charter*," p. 59.

6. Raymonde Folco, President of the *Conseil des communautés culturelles et de l'immigration* in Montreal explicitly endorses the view that, on entering Canada, immigrants commit themselves to a "moral contract" with their new community. See "Allaire villipendé par le Conseil des communautés culturelles," *Le Devoir*, March 23, 1994.

7. See note 12 below.

8. In 1964, in "Federalism, Nationalism, and Reason," in the context of a discussion of the nature of the federal state, Pierre Trudeau wrote:

> Federalism is by its very essence a compromise and a pact. It is a compromise in the sense that when national consensus on *all* things is not desirable or cannot readily obtain, the area of consensus is reduced in order that consensus on *some* things be reached. It is a pact or quasi-treaty in the sense that the terms of that compromise cannot be changed unilaterally...[T]he nation is based on a social contract, the terms of which each new generation of citizens is free to accept tacitly, or to reject openly."

See Pierre Elliott Trudeau, *Federalism and the French Canadians* (Toronto: Macmillan, 1968), pp. 191-92.

9. For such an argument, see Ian Macdonald, "Group Rights," *Philosophical Papers*, Vol. 18, no. 2 (September 1989), pp. 117-36.

10. See Michael Hartney, "Some Confusions Concerning Collective Rights," *The Canadian Journal of Law and Jurisprudence*, Vol. 4, no. 2 (July 1991), pp. 293-314; Macdonald, "Group Rights," p. 117; and Tom Campbell, *Justice* (New Jersey: Humanities Press International, 1988), pp. 36-54.

11. Our discussion here echoes at many points that of Will Kymlicka in "Group Representation in Canadian Politics," in F. Leslie Seidle (ed.), *Equity and Community: The Charter, Interest Advocacy and Representation* (Montreal: Institute for Research on Public Policy, 1993), pp. 61-89.

12. They are *quasi*-permanent because the political community is evolving and changing. Some of these defining features, or aspects of them, may eventually disappear. At the same time, new ones may emerge. The recognition of Canadians' multicultural heritage in section 27 of the Charter is a case in point. The interests to which that clause is addressed are clearly collective ones, as can be seen by testing them against the two criteria set out in the text: (a) the promotion of, say, Sikh Canadians' special interests as a multicultural community obviously requires the existence of a Sikh community; and (b) use of section 27 to advance a certain interpretation of the Charter – e.g., that the freedom of religion guaranteed under section 2(a) gives Sikh RCMP officers the right to wear turbans – represents an appeal to the particular historical and cultural practices of the Sikh community and of its special place in the larger Canadian political community. As such, section 27 adds a new dimension to federal pluralism.

13. The "interests" referred to here are ones that someone might argue are important enough to be protected by law. Thus those who agree with point 4 (p. 72) need not deny that there are *any* collective interests. They need only deny that there are any that merit protection under the law. In other words, they deny that there are any collective moral rights.

14. Janet Hiebert, "The Dilemma of the Charter: Is Judicial Deference Appropriate?", paper prepared for the Canadian Political Science Association 66th Annual Meeting (Calgary, June 12-14, 1994), pp. 5-6.

15. *R. v. Oakes* [1986] 1 S.C.R. 103.

16. Hiebert, "The Dilemma of the Charter," p. 6.

17. Hiebert, "The Dilemma of the Charter" is a lucid and informative discussion of the Court's struggle with this dilemma.

18. See Andrew Lokan, "The Rise and Fall of Doctrine Under Section 1 of the Charter," *Ottawa Law Review*, Vol. 24, no. 1 (1992), p. 177.

19. *Edmonton Journal v. Alberta (A.G.)* [1989] 2 S.C.R. 1326, at 1355-56.

20. A similar position is considered in Lokan, "The Rise and Fall of Doctrine," pp. 184-92.

21. See chapter 5 of this volume.

APPLYING THE CONCEPTS

7

LIBERALISM AND
THE INHERENT RIGHT TO
SELF-GOVERNMENT

The Inherent Right to Self-Government

In Canada, most organizations representing Aboriginal peoples claim for their constituents an inherent right to self-government. Outside the native community, there has been much confusion over what this means. Some fear such a right may imply full state sovereignty; others see it as akin to municipal government. In a 1992 report on constitutional reform, the Assembly of First Nations (AFN) explained self-government with a quote from one of its members:

> What is self-government? It means that a group governs itself. It makes its own laws, based on its values, customs, and culture. And our cultures are diverse, our languages are diverse...[1]

In the meta-vision of Canadian federalism we are developing, respect for the cultural diversity of First Nations is central. Nevertheless, the claim to an inherent right to self-government raises at least three important questions for our project:

- What measures are required to accommodate the needs of First Nations?
- How much diversity can be accommodated without undermining the essential interests of the larger Canadian community?
- Does an inherent right to self-government imply a right to secede?

In this chapter we address these questions. Regarding the first, we believe our approach to diversity is flexible enough to accommodate the needs of Aboriginal peoples. Regarding the second, we argue that a commitment by all governments (including Aboriginal ones) to respect individual freedom and equality is essential to the integrity of the Canadian political community. Regarding the third, we believe the right to self-government does not imply a right to secede. In any event, secession is not a viable option for the vast number of native communities in Canada; and few probably even want it. The real task is to identify the special needs of native communities in order to assess, in each case, what form self-government should take in order to meet them effectively.

IS LIBERALISM A FORM OF COLONIALISM?

As a political and moral theory, liberalism has not done justice to cultural diversity. Some in the Aboriginal community may therefore look with suspicion on our project of integrating liberalism and federalism. There is a strong belief among Aboriginal people that "[a]s long as institutions are controlled by non-Native people, non-Native concepts and philosophies, [First Peoples] cannot expect any justice from them."[2]

We will not discuss in detail First Nations' representation in institutions. We do want to consider, however, the question of what, exactly, counts as "non-Native concepts and philosophies." Do these include liberal principles? If so, does this mean that institutions of Aboriginal self-government or an Aboriginal system of justice might be based on non-liberal principles? In the eyes of at least some, this seems to be the case.

For example, the Royal Commission on Aboriginal Peoples recounts the presentation of one native spokesperson who "outlined an Aboriginal code of justice based on research into customary ways." The spokesperson understood the basis of the traditional system as follows: "When people broke the rules, the Indian system would try to bring them back into the community to teach them about their problem...Corrective measures could include gossip, shunning, shaming, and banishment..."[3] It is a serious question whether or how far such practices would accord with liberal principles of justice.

The Commission cites further testimony suggesting that some Aboriginal people view the principles on which Canada's political institutions and system of justice rest as essential to neither the institutions of self-government nor an Aboriginal system of justice: "Some Aboriginal people who spoke to the Commission said that the inherent right of self-government means they can govern themselves in any way they see fit, without reference to Canada."[4]

Differences over the relationship between liberal principles and self-government erupted during the Canada Round when a debate broke out over whether self-government should be subject to the Canadian Charter of Rights and Freedoms. Some native leaders – in particular, those from the AFN – maintained that it should not, while the Canadian government, many non-Aboriginal commentators and the Native Women's Association of Canada insisted that it should be. The debate was further fuelled by arguments that key sections of the Charlottetown Accord would have exempted Aboriginal self-government from the Charter.[5]

In their arguments, native spokespersons often linked the issue to the respect for cultural diversity. It is wrong, they said, for one culture to impose its values and traditions on another. The Charter was said to reflect a "Eurocanadian" perspective; forcing it on First Nations was described as colonialism. Aboriginal leaders who opposed application of the Charter acknowledged that it may contain a good formulation of universal rights for non-native society, but maintained that it is not the place of that society to decide whether it serves the interests of native peoples.

We do not view our insistence on respect for the liberal principles in the Charter as colonialism. On the contrary, we believe that, when properly understood, these principles are consistent with the legitimate aims and aspirations of Aboriginal peoples. In order to clarify our views on this, we want to consider the following question: if Aboriginal peoples do have a right to self-government, on what is it based?

TWO ARGUMENTS FOR THE RIGHT TO SELF-GOVERNMENT

Two general arguments seem to be advanced by First Peoples in support of an inherent right of self-government. The first begins by noting that Aboriginal peoples were self-governing long before non-natives arrived. Subsequent treaties, it continues, were viewed by First Nations as documents of coexistence – that is, they were agreements concluded between separate nations, which Aboriginal leaders say is confirmed in treaties, by the Royal Proclamation of 1763 and in common law.[6] First Peoples claim that they have never relinquished their sovereign rights as peoples or their lands. Therefore, on the principle that "[n]o people can be governed without their consent,"[7] they conclude that they have a right to govern themselves. We can call this the *consent argument*.

The second line of argument alludes to the long history First Nations have as distinct communities. It points to the diversity of their cultural traditions, some of which have existed for thousands of years. The practices, values, languages, myths and religions that make up these cultures are thought to constitute "ways of life" that are fundamentally different from those of non-native society. Preserving the integrity of such ways of life, it is argued, is crucial to the well-being of the members of the community. They depend upon it to help them develop a sense of who they are and what their lives are about. Indeed, in the view of the AFN, it is the "loss of land, language, culture, spirituality" that has "led to the loss of identity, to self-hatred, low self-esteem, abuse..."[8]

In this view, the special cultural needs of the community cannot be adequately managed by outsiders. It is the members of the community who best understand their own ways and hence who must restore the "spiritual balance." This means governing themselves according to their own methods, traditions and customs – *whether or not these methods are in keeping with federal or provincial laws and policies."*[9] We can call this the *cultural differences argument*.

Regarding the consent argument, we agree that moral and political ties, rights and duties between peoples (or individuals) can arise or be rescinded by agreement. We also agree that, as nations with treaties, Aboriginal Peoples do not stand in the same moral or legal relationship to the Canadian state as the descendants of, say, United Empire Loyalists or Italian immigrants.

Regarding the cultural differences argument, we accept – indeed, we ourselves have insisted – that a sense of community is crucial to the health of a society. We also accept that, in the case of native peoples, the promotion of community is tied to the vitality of their own languages and their distinct cultural traditions. Finally, we accept that decisions about how best to promote these interests should, where practicable, be the responsibility of the community.

These points we regard as consistent with the meta-vision we are developing. To admit them is in effect to admit that First Peoples have an inherent right to self-government, and, insofar as treaty rights have not been respected, a just grievance against the Canadian state. But, as we argue below, acknowledging that native peoples are "nations" or that they have an inherent right to self-government does *not* imply a right to full territorial sovereignty as, for example, Mohawk leaders on the Akwesasne reserve claim. Nor does it imply that a self-governing native community is free to base its political institutions or system of justice on tradition, rather than liberal principles, whenever there is a conflict between the two.

If we agree that there is an inherent right to self-government, we do not view it as a *tabula rasa* onto which a self-governing First Nation may inscribe whatever political system or laws it wishes. The interpretation of this right is, in our view, subject to at least two over-arching conditions: a respect for individual freedom and equality; and a respect for the historical context in which the right is claimed.

Individual Autonomy as the Foundation of the Claim to the Inherent Right

What do Aboriginal peoples see as the source of the inherent right to self-government? They often say this right was "bestowed by the Creator."[10] At the very least, this suggests that the legitimacy or authority of the right is thought to supersede the legitimacy of the *legal* authority (defined in section 91(24) of the Constitution Act, 1867) the Canadian government presently has with respect to Aboriginal People. To put this in the context of our own analysis, we would say the inherent right is an expression of what in the last chapter we called a *collective interest* – an extremely important and basic one which, for that reason, we agree to call a *moral right*.

Let us begin by pointing out that the two general arguments we said native leaders advance in support of the claim to an inherent right, while necessary, are not sufficient to establish its (moral) legitimacy. For the Aboriginal leaders to claim for their peoples a right to exercise autonomy, a third condition must be met: there must be some indication that the claim has the genuine support of the people. Without this, the claim would only represent the views of a group of political elites whose claim to "speak for the nation" would be open to question. We are *not*, of course, denying that such support exists. But the point has implications that have not been fully appreciated.

Political activists who want to advance a claim to political autonomy for their people usually engage in "political consciousness raising." First, activists try to convince the people that they constitute a *nation* – that is, a cohesive group with a common cultural and linguistic tradition. Second, they try to convince the group that, as a nation, it has a right (and a desire) to promote its common interests, rather than entrusting them to "outsiders." Consciousness-raising strategies are usually carried out through a campaign of speeches, demonstrations, rallies and publications aimed at inciting the people to become politically active in ways that support the cause.

What is at issue when activists invite individual members of a group to support their political cause in this way?

At least two things are implied. First, in seeking the group's support, the activists acknowledge that the individual members of the community have the capacity to judge for themselves the merits of the arguments being advanced. Second, the activists are also acknowledging that the group's willingness to endorse their arguments and goals is necessary if these are to have validity with "outsiders." This suggests a kind of social contract between the leaders and the members of the group: the latter lend their support to the cause – thereby legitimizing it – while the former agree that their legitimacy as spokespersons for the group has been derived from a recognition of, and a commitment to respect, the viewpoint of the individual members of the community. This is the seminal idea behind the idea of the consent of the governed. It is inspired by the liberal vision of individuals as free and equal citizens.

These reflections suggest that the force behind Aboriginal leaders' claim to a right of self-government cannot be divorced from liberal convictions about the need to respect the freedom and equality of individual members of native communities. If the claim is to be taken seriously, it is in part because many of the Aboriginal leaders who advance it seem genuinely to speak for the people they represent.[11] As the Royal Commission notes, "self-government is seen almost universally by Aboriginal people as the way forward and as an essential element in the new relationship they envisage with the rest of Canada."[12] But if the leaders' legitimacy is based on an implicit commitment to respect the individual freedom of the members of their communities, that commitment must be reflected in the practices and institutions of self-government. To do otherwise would be to violate the terms of the social contract with their own members and hence to undermine their own legitimacy.

There appears to be a subtle irony here, namely that one of native leaders' main arguments to protect their cultural identity from assimilation to our Eurocanadian one seems to be built on key concepts central to the European philosophical and moral tradition. Indeed, one finds liberal ideas scattered throughout native leaders' discussions of self-government.[13]

Aboriginal leaders will reply here that, when they appear to endorse such "liberal" principles, they are really returning to their own roots. They often claim that their own societies were based upon similar values and practices. Thus, in a discussion of the Charter, the Royal Commission reminds us that "First Peoples are no strangers to the doctrines of freedom and equality that animate the Charter." The Commission then supports this view with a quote from the French historian Charlevoix who, in 1744, gave the following description of life in native societies:

> Born free and independent, they have a horror of the least shadow of a despotic power, but they stray rarely from certain usages and principles founded on good sense...In this country all Humanity believes itself equally men, and in Man what they most esteem is Man. No distinction of right, no prerogative of rank.[14]

The Commission concludes that: "The principles that animate [the Charter] arguably have multiple roots, then, spreading deep into both Aboriginal and non-Aboriginal societies."[15]

This may be so. If it is, this is a very welcome and positive sign, not only because it narrows the supposed gap between liberals and some Aboriginal peoples, but also because it accords with what we argue elsewhere in this book – namely, that certain values seem to be universal and that, insofar as an approach to politics is based upon them, it recognizes the importance of drawing a basic distinction between respect for the individual and the authority of custom, tradition, culture or race. If it is true that native societies developed an approach to government similar to the one we support, but centuries before it existed, this should be seen as strong evidence that what we have been calling liberalism is *not* just a parochial European view of politics, but one that rests on a respect for universal – that is, human – interests.

Still, even if native leaders agree that an approach to politics based upon universal principles is the right one, this does not yet solve the problem of cultural diversity. It is plain that, like us, they have not resolved in a clear and satisfactory way how individual freedom and equality are to be reconciled with the special historical and cultural interests of their communities. This is reflected in the ambivalence of their own political discourse, which often swings back and forth between talk of respect for human rights and passionate professions of faith in traditionalism. So the question remains: insofar as traditional forms of government in some native societies do depart from liberal norms, how far should the respect for that diversity go?

CONTEXTUALIZING THE INHERENT RIGHT TO SELF-GOVERNMENT

In fact, the question is not as perplexing as it may seem. We have argued that the right to self-government implies a respect for individual freedom and equality. We have also noted that native peoples often insist that this is in keeping with their own traditions of government. If both points are accepted, the real question now is a practical one: what sort of mechanism should regulate the citizen-state relationship in self-governing communities? More specifically: is the Charter adequate to the task of defining the commitment to individual freedom and equality in such communities? We believe it is. Perhaps the best way to explain our position is to begin with an example.

On a number of occasions during the Canada Round, the AFN's Grand Chief, Ovide Mercredi, gave the following example to help explain the organization's resistance to the idea that self-government should be subject to the Charter. He recounted that in traditional Mohawk society tribal leaders were chosen by clan mothers. Mercredi expressed concern that, if native self-government were subject to the Charter, the courts might find this practice inconsistent with the democratic rights in sections 3 and 4.[16] But, he asked rhetorically, who are non-natives to tell Mohawks not to use this method of leadership selection if that is what their people want?

It is noteworthy that this defence of the clan mother system ends with the comment "if that is what their people want." It is hard to take this any other way than as a tacit appeal to one of the three basic rights embodied in sections 3 and 4 of the Charter, namely, the consent of the governed. If Chief Mercredi also agreed that this consent should be subject to periodic review by the people who grant it (a second condition implied by these sections), we suspect few liberals would take exception to the use of these traditional leadership selection practices.

Of course, there still remains the third condition implied in sections 3 and 4 of the Charter – the right to stand for office – but we also believe non-native Canadians could be persuaded to agree with Mercredi that, if the community democratically chooses to forgo this option in order to preserve the clan mother system, and if that commitment is subject to periodic review, they should be allowed to do so.

One possibility is that the courts might find that a legal right to self-government exists in section 35 of the Constitution Act, 1982, as many native leaders, the Royal Commission and the federal government all claim. A second is that this right becomes entrenched. Either way, we would argue that this legal right to self-government: (a) should be subject to the Charter; and that this means (b) while section 25 is not a "shield" against the Charter, it can still be used as a "filter."[17]

We argued that in claiming a *moral* right to self-government on behalf of First Nations, Aboriginal leaders implicitly commit themselves to the principle of respect for the individual freedom and equality of the members of their communities. We also noted that many Aboriginal leaders view this commitment as consistent with traditional forms of government. This seems to us to imply that the institutions of self-government must[18] reflect what we have been calling liberal principles. If so, the argument advanced by some that section 25 of the Charter shields self-government from Charter application seems very questionable.[19] That would only be the case if the "existing aboriginal and treaty rights" in section 35 included forms of government and practices that fail to respect those sections of the Charter designed to protect various aspects of individual freedom and equality.[20] But, if our analysis is correct, this is not so.

However, while section 25 cannot serve as a "shield" against Charter application, there is no reason it cannot serve as a "filter" – that is, insofar as the "existing aboriginal and treaty rights" in section 35 protect culturally distinct practices and values that are nevertheless consistent with the commitment to respect individual freedom and equality, then the application of the Charter to self-governing native communities must be consistent with them. Section 25 would thus play a role for native communities similar to the one we have suggested section 1 might play for concerns over language in Quebec.

But what if the courts do not find that an inherent right exists in section 35 and governments do not entrench one? If the meta-vision we are proposing is accepted, respect for Aboriginal Peoples' cultural distinctness will be understood as a key part of the commitment of federalism. In effect, this would amount to a strong argument that, whatever else it may include, the reference to existing Aboriginal rights in section 35(1) of the Constitution Act, 1982 implies a recognition of, and respect for, the particular cultural and linguistic needs of different native communities. This in itself could be construed as an instruction to use section 25 to ensure interpretation of the Charter is consistent with the special needs of native communities. Indeed, insofar as the federalist principle of the respect for diversity defended in this book implies a community right to some control, where practicable, over the interests at stake,[21] it is in the end not all that different from the idea of a (moral) right to self-government. For it can be appealed to as a justification for greater control over decision-making power. The (moral) right to self-government and the respect for cultural diversity are both ways of underlining particular ranges of community-based interests that play a special role in Confederation.

We wish to draw two main conclusions from this discussion. One is that the whole debate over whether or not basic liberal rights are Eurocentric is a bit of a red herring. Native self-government should be based on a respect for individual freedom and equality. The "debate" over whether the rights that flow from this commitment ought to be called liberal rights or human rights or something else is, as far as we are concerned, purely academic. The second conclusion is that the Charter is consistent with native peoples' legitimate aspirations for self-government.

Some Aboriginal people will doubt this second claim. We cannot anticipate all the cases and objections that might be raised. But, to those who doubt that the Charter can be made consistent with First Nations' commitment to freedom and equality, we reply with a question: what changes do they think are needed in the existing Charter to make it (a) consistent with their own needs and aspirations; but (b) still committed to individual freedom and equality?

This is not a rhetorical question. It is earnestly posed. The task of integrating freedom and equality with diversity is a deep and complex one, and we think the liberal tradition has not done justice to the issues. Perhaps, then, Aboriginal communities do have legitimate interests to which the Charter would remain insensitive, even if section 25 were used as a filter. But it is not clear what they are. In the meantime, we presume that the societies First Nations wish to build are both the same as and different from that of non-native Canadians.

They are the same in that they must respect the rule of law, the consent of the governed and basic human rights such as the right (within reasonable limits) to leave and re-enter the community, freedom of association, speech and conscience, and the equality of men and women. They are different in that the different practices, traditions, rituals, beliefs, languages, myths and history that unite the members of a given Aboriginal community may result in important differences regarding how these rights are to be understood and applied. Thus it may be the case that, say, certain traditional values in Inuit society will lead the courts to conclude that preventing practice X in that society is a "reasonable limit" on the freedom of expression, while in, say, Mohawk society it is not.[22] In short, native societies will differ from non-native society (and from one another) at the level of their cultures and languages; but all will overlap at the level of their respect for common humanity.

DEFINING THE SCOPE OF THE INHERENT RIGHT

We have suggested that the respect for individual freedom and equality is one of two over-arching conditions to which the inherent right should be subject. The second was the historical context in which the right is claimed. What does this mean?

We restrict ourselves to two points. First, the inherent right of self-government does not imply a right to secession. Second, the implementation of this right must be worked out within the context of the Canadian Constitution. Let us begin with those who insist that First Peoples have a right to govern themselves in any way they see fit, without reference to Canada.[23]

This claim, it should be noted, is *not* derived from the inherent right of self-government, but rather from a claimed right to *self-determination*. Many native leaders now insist they have such a right. The Royal Commission explains the distinction between these two rights this way: "Self-determination is a broader concept than self-government. It rests upon the willing consent of a people to the institutions that manage its society. Self-government is one of the means by which self-determination can be achieved."[24] Some, though by no means all, Aboriginal leaders explicitly link the right to self-determination to a right to secede.[25] They justify this on the ground that they are sovereign peoples and that section 1 of the United Nations Covenant on Social, Economic and Cultural Rights, to which Canada is a signatory, states that all peoples have a right of self-determination. Do First Peoples in Canada, a sovereign country with a Constitution more than 125 years old, have such a right? We think not.

In 1970 the General Assembly of the United Nations passed the Declaration on Principles of International Law concerning Friendly Relations and Cooperation among States. This reaffirmed the right of self-determination of peoples, but it also stated that the exercise of the right should not lead to the dismemberment or threaten the territorial integrity of a state. Secession or separation of an Aboriginal community from Canada would obviously affect its territorial integrity.

Just as there is no basis in international law for a right of self-determination involving a right to secede, so there is no basis in the Constitution of Canada. There is nothing surprising about that. So far as we are aware, with the exception of the former Soviet Union, no constitution of any country contains any provision for secession by a people or a region. Again, that is not surprising. A state is a political community in which there is (especially after more than a century of existence) an interweaving of rights, interests and obligations shared by the people who comprise it. There can be no constitutionally declared right by some of the people within the community to leave it without taking into account the interests, rights and concerns of the people of the community as a whole.

The question whether, in such circumstances, there would be a moral or political basis for secession or separation is another matter. If an Aboriginal people within the political community of Canada were clearly to indicate its wish to leave it and accept the consequences of its separation from the rest of Canada, a complex question would arise on which agreement would have to be reached. If none could be achieved, and if separation without agreement were to be insisted on, it is impossible to know what would happen. Apart from the question of a right, legal or moral, any possible secession would raise the question of international recognition for a new state. Recognition by other states is not a matter of law. It is a political and discretionary act of the governments of other countries to decide.

In our judgement, raising the issues of self-determination or secession is neither constructive nor helpful to the question of Aboriginal self-government. For better or for worse, the political fates of native and non-native communities are linked. Aboriginal peoples are part of the Canadian political landscape. The search for a solution to their legitimate place in Canada is part of a search for a solution to a set of interrelated challenges in Confederation. Whatever "self-determination" or "self-government" means, it certainly does not imply a right to act in any way a community wishes, without regard for the legitimate interests of other communities. Nor does it imply that the economic, financial and institutional support in place prior to separation or secession would continue unaffected. New relationships would need to be articulated between the new state and what would remain of the old one on the basis of their respective interests.

In any event, the question of a right to secession is largely moot since, as the Commission notes, "[m]ost [native spokespersons] agree...that the idea of separate Aboriginal nation states is neither practical nor beneficial for Aboriginal peoples."[26] We take it as given that self-government has to be worked out within the context of the Canadian community. The real task, we think, is to identify the special needs of native communities in order to assess where self-government will be an effective way of meeting them.

In seeking to define self-government, there seem to us three aspects of the Aboriginal issue that exert a compelling claim on Canadians' sense of fairness and justice. The first is Aboriginal peoples' claim – supported by past practice, as well as treaties, common law and the Royal Proclamation of 1763 – to a special place in the Canadian federation. We argued in chapter 2 that federalism was aimed at protecting the interests of the French- and English-speaking linguistic communities and of regional communities. We also think the unique historical position of native peoples establishes them as what, in chapter 6, we called a "federal" community. In other words, First Nations have a special right to have their integrity protected by the Constitution.

The second important aspect of the Aboriginal issue is the appalling condition of many native communities. Statistics on the high rates of unemployment, illiteracy, violence, child abuse, alcohol and substance abuse, suicide and infant mortality in many native communities have been widely publicized in recent years. In addition, there are currently hundreds of outstanding claims filed by native communities with the Department of Indian Affairs. These include land claims, compensation for dislocation and grievances over the failure to meet treaty obligations and to deliver promised services. All of this provides ample evidence to support Aboriginal peoples' claim that their interests as a community are not well served by the *status quo;* and hence that a new relationship is needed.

The third aspect of the Aboriginal issue that needs to be addressed is cultural security. Insofar as the integrity of native communities and the well-being of their members depend upon the existence of a vibrant, flourishing cultural identity, we think the desire to protect and promote a distinct cultural identity provides a basis for seeking control over certain decision-making powers.

Reflecting on these three aspects of the Aboriginal issue leads us to the conclusion that the strongest reason for self-government is that it is the most hopeful way of improving the overall well-being of native peoples in Confederation. In spite of the failure of the Charlottetown Accord, which would have entrenched the inherent right to self-government, the Liberal government of Jean Chrétien has taken the position that the right is implicit in section 35 of the Constitution Act, 1982. As should be apparent, we agree with this. The question now is how to implement that right. The practical difficulties are formidable and cannot be swept under the rug:

- There are four major classes of Aboriginal peoples: Inuit, status Indians, non-status Indians and Métis. These classes themselves subdivide many times.
- An increasing number of Aboriginal people live in urban communities where they form a minority intermingled with a majority that is not Aboriginal.
- Non-status Indians and many Métis have no land base. Hence the form self-government will take for them will have to be very different from that of status Indians.
- Among Indian bands, variations with respect to wealth, land, population size and proximity to non-native communities, as well as culture, language, goals and needs, are sometimes enormous.
- There are vast differences in the degree of First Nations' existing institutional and administrative infrastructure as well as professional capacity.
- In some communities the paternalistic approaches of the past have left social and cultural structures badly damaged.
- In many communities a culture of dependency has developed that must be overcome.
- There is some ambiguity between the words "community" and "First Nation." Is every band to be considered a "nation" if it wishes? Or, where a number of bands living in the same region have a common tribal history, should the focus be on negotiating with the entire group, perhaps with the goal of establishing a kind of "cluster nation?"
- The distinction between on- and off-reserve band members seems to be creating two classes of status Indians: community members and non-community members.
- Divergences of legal and political status within communities as a result of the 1985 amendments to the *Indian Act* (Bill C-31) may greatly complicate the political and social structure of Aboriginal communities in the years ahead.
- Many reserves have people living on them who are not, or are only partly, native. As a result, there are already various (social and legal) levels of community membership.
- Some bands have treaties; others do not.

We cannot address all these issues here. Space limits us to making a few key points about the approach we advocate to establish self-government for bands with reserve lands.

SELF-GOVERNMENT FROM THE BOTTOM UP

For First Nations peoples on reserves, self-government means assuming control over program funding and decision-making power. In most cases, this will happen gradually. At some point along the path, however, further transfers of power to a particular band will require that it "opt out" of the Indian Act and establish its own self-government agreement. Eventually, the Act should be replaced by a series of such agreements. These will be based on a set of common principles that define the role of a "third order" of government while remaining flexible enough to allow each First Nation to tailor its own agreement to its needs and aspirations.

Federal programs for Indians are already undergoing a major shift. While in the past benefits were often delivered directly to individuals from Crown agencies, programs are increasingly managed by Indian bands. Over 80 percent of the programs of the Department of Indian Affairs are now focussed at the community level. Community involvement ranges from a simple administrative role, to graduated control over program design and delivery, to block-funding arrangements, to full-scale self-government agreements.

However, where input into or control over program design exists, it is often constrained by the Indian Act. At the same time, moving beyond the Act raises many issues. Many communities are not yet ready to substitute the Act with a full-scale self-government agreement and may not be for some years. Its sudden disappearance would leave them with no legal framework defining their rights or federal responsibilities to them. In such cases, what is needed is an orderly transfer of power leading to the emergence of a form of self-government that reflects the needs and interests of the community.

The federal government also has concerns about moving too quickly. For one thing, many First Nations have neither the institutional capacity nor the human resources to implement self-government. For another, too great a transfer too fast could lead to inequity. For various reasons, band councils may develop eligibility criteria for programs that restrict access in ways that some think unfair. For example, on some reserves membership codes prevent the children of certain band members who are married to non-status Indians from gaining band membership, even though they may have spent their entire lives on the reserve.[27] What counts as equitable access?

In theory, in a self-governing First Nation, it is the responsibility of local decision makers to set criteria for access that reflect the community's understanding of, and commitment to, the equality of its members. If the leadership is representative and responsible, it will have to answer to the people for policies that do not reflect their interests and values as a community. In this way, the fairness of the decision-making procedures guarantees the fairness of the eligibility criteria.

Thus, where full self-government is a reality, the equity question should not be an issue for the federal government. Each community should define the terms of its commitment to equality for itself. However, as noted, for most First Nations self-government is more a goal than a reality. Appealing to decision-making procedures as a way of ensuring equity therefore may only beg the question, leading some in the community to ask whether the procedures are really representative and responsible, and who should rightly be called a member of the community or nation.

For many Aboriginal persons, these issues have not been settled. Getting to that point may take years. Nevertheless, control over funding and programs is being transferred now. In the interim, the federal government remains responsible for the welfare of those who depend on its support. It must ensure that their interests are not overlooked or disregarded in the move to self-government.

In short, the federal government has a responsibility to take a position on some of these contentious issues.[28] It would be wrong to brush them off as internal matters in the age of self-government. Self-governing communities are not independent states. They are part of the larger Canadian community in which they are embedded. The federal government continues to have responsibilities to their members as Canadian citizens. But protecting and promoting their interests as Canadian citizens could have important consequences. For example, it could lead to delays in the full transfer of funds until the community's institutional capacity becomes more developed. It could also lead to attaching conditions to program transfers regarding eligibility criteria. Where such conditions are included, they must be arrived at in a way that is viewed as rational and fair, rather than paternalistic, by both the individuals and the communities whose interests are at stake. How is this to be done?

The answer may lie in the development of *devolution strategies* – that is, arrangements by which control over funds, program administration and design and decision-making power would pass to a particular community in a series of stages. Devolution would be used as a catalyst to develop the community's institutional capacity and human resources, as well as to forge political institutions and practices that are generally viewed as legitimate by those living under them. A devolution strategy might include such elements as a broad timetable for assuming increased control over programs; administrative or other conditions placed on the control of funds or a program; and the inclusion of certain objectives in program design.

The theoretical endpoint of a devolution strategy is a self-governing arrangement that reflects the particular needs, goals and circumstances of the community and its members. The terms and conditions of that arrangement need not be stated at the beginning of the process. On the contrary, each First Nation should be allowed to find its own equilibrium with the larger Canadian community in which it is embedded. The conception of self-government should be expected to evolve and change as a community moves along the path. However, when a First Nation believes it has found an arrangement that suits its needs and aspirations, and if it is able to assume the administrative and other responsibilities associated with it, it should have the right to "finalize" the agreement. That is, its members must feel confident (a) that they are now in control of their own future; and (b) that the arrangements will not be unilaterally altered by forces outside the community.

Regarding the first point, a community must be able to "opt out" of the Indian Act, if it wishes, once it reaches a degree and form of self-government that both governments and its members consider workable and fair. It must, in short, be able to cast off the vestiges of paternalism that the Act represents. Regarding the second point, self-government agreements need constitutional protection. As long as they have only the status of statute laws they will be at the whim of Parliament, which could unilaterally alter them at its discretion. This does not provide a secure enough basis on which to build a self-governing community. Unfortunately, the Constitution presently lacks a mechanism to provide protection for such agreements. An amendment to the Constitution to entrench such a mechanism is therefore both necessary and desirable within the not-too-distant future, if the project of self-government is not to get stalled.

Who would define the terms and conditions of a devolution strategy? These would be the result of negotiations between federal authorities and community leaders. But to ensure that attached conditions were not the expression of lingering paternalism, they would have to meet a two-fold test. First, they must plausibly be seen as an effective means of promoting values and objectives that all agree are essential to the goal of self-government. Second, they must be designed to help the community overcome, or accommodate, some condition that presents an obstacle to the realization of self-government.

In effect, this means that discussions between federal officials and a First Nation on the transfer of funds and decision-making power should take place against the backdrop of a meta-vision that defines the over-arching objectives and values of self-government. This meta-vision would be based on a balanced commitment to five over-arching objectives:

- respect for culture;
- social equality;
- individual freedom;
- effective governance; and
- economic non-dependence.

These five objectives would serve as points of reference for assessing a community's current position along the road to autonomy, its immediate needs and a strategy to promote development of the values, institutions and practices on which full self-government would eventually rest. In short, they would provide a framework for developing a devolution strategy and for applying the two-part test.

Suppose, for example, that a First Nation had adopted a highly restrictive membership code based on blood quanta. Suppose, further, that this code excluded five percent of the population living on the reserve who, on other reasonable grounds, argued that they had a right to membership. In such a case, the federal government might take the position that the community's pursuit of its cultural objectives was threatening to overwhelm its commitment to social equality. It might therefore argue, as a condition for transferring control of, say, funding for post-secondary education, that the excluded five percent be given reasonable access to the program until a resolution of the issue had been reached.

By "effective governance" we mean the ability of a community fairly and efficiently to exercise powers, administer programs and manage resources. Deciding what conditions, if any, might reasonably be attached to the transfer of control over certain programs or funds or decision-making powers in order to promote effective governance will involve the examination of a wide range of practical issues. These include the location of the band; the extent of its land base; its wealth and population size; the level of development of its existing institutions; and the impact self-government will have on other non-native communities in the vicinity as well as on provincial and federal governments. As with each of the other objectives, of course, "effective governance" must be seen as part of a workable balance among all five.

While few communities have the resources to sustain on their own an acceptable level of services for their members, the high debt and deficit will put the federal government under increasing pressure to reduce rather than increase expenditures. Devolution strategies should therefore help communities evolve as quickly as possible toward "non-dependence" on federal funding. In many cases, this means members will often have to work off-reserve, maybe for extended periods of time.

This issue of transience could pose one of the most serious obstacles to a community's efforts to preserve its distinctive cultural and linguistic heritage. In response, many communities may need to start early on to develop a policy on mobility rights for members. This would specify which benefits are portable and when; and the conditions under which absenteeism would lead to loss of membership. Many self-governing communities will also need to develop their own membership codes or, in some cases, to amend those they now have. The terms and conditions of membership must not only be perceived as legitimate by those with strong ties to the band; they must also be flexible enough to permit new policies on emigration and immigration in response to changing demographic needs.

Even with such new policies, the objective of economic non-dependence will take many years to achieve and, in many cases, may not be achievable at all without a sub-structure of support comparable to but possibly broader than the equalization payments that now underwrite the provision of essential services by "have-not" provinces. An amendment to section 36 of the Constitution Act, 1982 might be desirable at some future date, but with adaptation to the special circumstances of some Aboriginal communities. Including the objective of non-dependence is, first and foremost, a way of emphasizing the need to avoid the development of a culture of dependence.

In conclusion, three observations seem to follow from our examination of the inherent right to self-government in this chapter. First, it is not a *tabula rasa* onto which native leaders may freely inscribe whatever they will. It is a powerful and evocative image by which they have advanced a legitimate claim to adequate control over their communities in order to ensure the well-being of their members. Second, the form that self-government will take will vary, perhaps dramatically, across the country according to the peculiar needs and capacities of each community. Third, this diversity notwithstanding, the federal government and First Nations need to develop a common meta-vision for self-government based on a balanced promotion of five over-arching goals: social equality, respect for individual freedom, collective commitment to cultural renewal and development, effective governance and economic non-dependence.

Notes

1. Assembly of First Nations (AFN), *To the Source: Commissioners' Report of the First Nations Circle on Confederation* (Ottawa: Assembly of First Nations, 1992), p. 17.

2. AFN, *To the Source*, p. 16.

3. Royal Commission on Aboriginal Peoples, *Overview of the Second Round* (Ottawa: Minister of Supply and Services Canada, 1993), p. 57.

4. Royal Commission on Aboriginal Peoples, *Discussion Paper 2: Focusing the Dialogue* (Ottawa: Minister of Supply and Services Canada, 1993), p. 28.

5. See Anne F. Bayefsky, "The Effect of Aboriginal Self-Government on the Rights and Freedoms of Women" (Ottawa: Network on the Constitution, October 1992), pp. 1-2.

6. See, for example, Royal Commission on Aboriginal Peoples, *Partners in Confederation: Aboriginal Peoples, Self-Government, and the Constitution* (Ottawa: Minister of Supply and Services Canada, 1993), pp. 16, 31-41.

7. AFN, *To the Source*, p. 16.

8. AFN, *To the Source*, p. 10.

9. AFN, *To the Source*, p. 11 (emphasis in original).

10. See, for example, AFN, *To the Source*, p. 16.

11. We say "in part" because both the consent and cultural distinctiveness arguments remain crucial to the validity of the claim. This will be further discussed below.

12. Royal Commission on Aboriginal Peoples, *Exploring the Options: Overview of the Third Round* (Ottawa: Minister of Supply and Services Canada, 1993), p. 30.

13. For example, AFN, *To the Source*, refers to the need to respect "elementary principles of democracy" (p. 15), describes how "government must flow upward from the people to their leaders" (p. 16) and specifically links the concept of the inherent right with the principle of popular consent (p. 13).

14. Royal Commission, *Partners in Confederation*, p. 40.

15. Royal Commission, *Partners in Confederation*, p. 40.

16. These sections guarantee Canadian citizens the right to vote and stand for office in national and provincial elections, and that national and provincial elections will be held at least once every five years.

17. Section 25 of the Charter guarantees that it will not be construed in a way so as to "abrogate or derogate from any aboriginal, treaty or other rights or freedoms that pertain to the aboriginal peoples of Canada..."

18. The "must" here is used in a moral, rather than legal, sense.

19. The argument is discussed in Royal Commission, *Partners in Confederation*, p. 39.

20. Section 35 recognizes and affirms "existing aboriginal and treaty rights of the aboriginal peoples of Canada." There is, however, considerable uncertainty as to what is included under "existing" Aboriginal rights.

21. See chapter 6 of this volume.

22. Suppose, for example, that the Clan Mother system were implemented in Mohawk society in a way that was consistent with the Charter, as we suggested above. It is certainly conceivable that, say, when deliberating about the choice of a new leader, the Clan Mothers might be justified in limiting the freedom of the press in certain ways in order to ensure the integrity of the process.

23. See, for example, Royal Commission, *Exploring the Options: Overview of the Third Round*, pp. 29-30.

24. Royal Commission, *Focusing the Dialogue*, p. 20.

25. Royal Commission, *Overview of the Second Round*, p. 30.

26. Royal Commission, *Focusing the Dialogue*, p. 28.

27. See Stewart Clatworthy and Anthony H. Smith, *Population Implications of the 1985 Amendments to the Indian Act* (Ottawa: Assembly of First Nations, December 1992), pp. 5-24.

28. A good account of the current state of the debate can be found in Dan Smith, *The Seventh Fire: The Struggle for Aboriginal Self-Government* (Toronto: Key Porter Books, 1993), pp. 8-32, 91-122.

8

NATIONALISM IN QUEBEC: THE OLD AND THE NEW

THE "NEW" NATIONALISM

Yesterday, Mr. Bouchard stressed that he is a moderate nationalist, not an extremist, saying that he does not place the nation above everything.[1]

There is something odd about this claim made by Lucien Bouchard during an official visit to the United States. What, we should ask, is a "moderate nationalist?"

Bouchard explains himself by contrasting moderate nationalism with "extreme forms of ethnic nationalism," such as that of the Bosnian Serbs. Presumably, then, moderate nationalists are those who do not use violence or oppression to achieve their goal of an independent state. In this sense, Bouchard surely is a moderate nationalist. But the account fails to convey the richness and ambiguity the term has acquired in Canadian politics.

For one thing, many *Québécois* who call themselves "moderate nationalists" do not support independence – or perhaps see it as a last resort. In their minds, the adjective "moderate" implies much more than a commitment to the use of democratic means in the quest for statehood. It identifies a particular approach to the politics of language and linguistic identity in Quebec, one which sees no inherent conflict between a profound attachment to "the nation" and membership in a larger, multi-national federal state.

In a perceptive article, *La Presse* editor Alain Dubuc contrasts what he calls the "old" and the "new" forms of nationalism in Quebec:

> The standard image of Quebec nationalism is that of an isolated Francophone people, an island awash in an Anglophone sea, requiring for its continued survival appropriate tools to ensure the protection and growth of its language, culture and identity...In the last quarter-century, however, another form of nationalism has emerged: one that considers the rest of Canada and Confederation not so much a threat to the survival of the French fact, but more a hindrance to its growth and fulfilment. Thus, once perceived to be a sword of Damocles, English-speaking Canada is now looked upon as a somewhat rusty ball and chain.[2]

Dubuc's description of the "new" nationalism comes closer to capturing the sense that the term "moderate nationalism" has in contemporary Quebec politics. In particular, the "new" or "moderate" nationalists do not see the preservation and promotion of "the nation" as the over-arching goal of politics. To be sure, they regard the unique identity of francophone Quebecers as a source of important political interests and aspirations. But there are other interests that must be weighed and balanced.

We agree that over the past quarter-century a new nationalism has been emerging in Quebec, one that reflects a changing view of language and identity. As a result, Quebec nationalism seems to be at a turning point. But the new direction remains unclear. The old nationalism is far from a spent force. Indeed, the two seem to be engaged in a political, intellectual and moral struggle, the outcome of which is, as yet, uncertain.

But it would be too simple just to equate the supporters of independence with the old nationalism, or supporters of federalism with the new nationalism. The battle lines are not that clear. The old and new nationalisms are more like two poles on a continuum than two sides of a coin. At the centre, as Dubuc's comments suggest, the distinction between old and new often seems to depend as much on emphasis, attitude and outlook, as on principles, objectives or party membership. Indeed, there are times when it is difficult to tell exactly what form someone is defending.[3] If there is a struggle under way between the two nationalisms, then, it is not just between federalists and *indépendantistes* (or confederalists). The struggle can often be seen at work within a single association, organization, political party and even within the ideas and arguments of the same person.

Perhaps the best way to approach the distinction is as a basis on which to define and defend Quebec's special interests and concerns as the only province or state in North America with a French-speaking majority. In any event, that is the tack we will take in this chapter. It leads us to conclude that, while the new nationalism is fast becoming the orthodox way for nationalists to think about Quebec's internal politics, when it comes to the question of Quebec's place in Confederation, many of the same nationalists still rely on outdated arguments based upon the old nationalism. It is, we conclude, time they squarely face this inconsistency.

GETTING A GRIP ON THE DISTINCTION

After 30 years of constitutional debates over Quebec's place in Confederation, the impending conclusion is that federalism can no longer accommodate the old nationalism, under which Quebec's cultural-linguistic distinctness was seen as all encompassing and, as a result, by which the whole of politics was assimilated to one point of view. Thus, during the Canada Round, Jean Allaire, former leader of the *Parti Action démocratique,* asked (apparently rhetorically): "Is it really possible to give a restrictive definition of culture and then separate culture and language from other types of powers, including economic powers?"[4]

This question helps us get a better grip on the difference between the old and new nationalisms. According to Allaire, the answer to the question is no. In his view, culture includes virtually everything. It is, he tells us, "a way to think, behave, work and even play: in a word, a way of life."[5] Quebec nationalists often make similar claims about the scope of language and national identity. But conceiving the concepts in this way opens a gap between French-speaking Quebecers and the rest of Canada that threatens to become unbridgeable precisely because these terms can be expanded, at will, to include almost anything. Their elasticity thus undermines attempts to identify a range of "shared interests" on which to build a stable federalist political culture in Canada.

But not all Quebec nationalists insist on an open-ended definition of terms such as "culture." For example, many speak instead of the need for "cultural sovereignty," a term that, while admittedly vague, is explicitly contrasted with others such as "economic integration." In this case, the term "culture" seems to be far less comprehensive. If an expression such as "cultural sovereignty" is to provide a foundation for a stable federalist political culture, it must be defined in a way that allows us to give a positive answer to Allaire's question. That is, it must permit us to use terms such as "culture" and "national identity" in a more disciplined way.

This latter approach is the one we think is taking shape at the core of the new or moderate nationalism. It recognizes the importance many Quebecers attach to the French language and to their distinct identity; and it agrees that these give rise to legitimate political aspirations. But it manages to keep them in perspective by distinguishing them from other important interests. This allows the idea of a linguistic or cultural identity to become relatively well defined.

Thus, from the point of view of the new nationalism, the cultural-linguistic distinctness of Quebec is a real issue; and the gap between the *Québécois* and the rest of Canada still exists. But this gap is, we will argue, a manageable one. As a result, the promotion of Quebec's distinct interests is consistent with its economic and political integration with the rest of Canada, that is, with federalism. By contrast, the outlook of the old nationalism, while it has evolved and changed over the years, still seeks to define Quebec's place in Confederation by reference to the open-ended version of these key concepts in the nationalist vocabulary. In order to clarify the similarities and differences between these two nationalisms, we want now to look briefly at the evolution of nationalist thought in Quebec.

THE CHANGING FACE OF QUEBEC NATIONALISM

The story of Quebec nationalism in the present century is a complex one, punctuated by a number of key events, including the conscription crisis of 1917, the Great Depression of the 1930s, another conscription crisis during the Second World War and the Quiet Revolution. The different periods in the nationalist movement and the diverse strands of thought that run through them – especially in the 1930s – make generalizations risky.

Still, it seems accurate to say that, in the half-century before the Quiet Revolution, the anchor of nationalist thought in Quebec was the concept of *la survivance:* as a sentiment, nationalism was viewed as a manifestation of the collective will to survive; as a political doctrine, it aimed at preserving the language, traditions, history and religion – in a word, the culture – of a people.[6] In this period, nationalism tended to be defensive, inward looking and conservative. One thinks especially of the provincialism of Abbé Lionel Groulx and, in a different way, that of Maurice Duplessis.[7]

Following the reforms of the Liberal government of Premier Jean Lesage in the early 1960s a powerful secularizing current swept Quebec's intellectual circles.[8] One of the first casualties of the new thinking was the Church. By mid-decade responsibility for the intellectual and spiritual leadership of "the nation" had shifted away from the clergy and onto academics, journalists, artists and the political elites. The tone of Quebec nationalism and Quebec politics changed dramatically.

But if the new secular trend in Quebec political thought began with a revolutionary overthrow of the *ancien régime,* the break with the past was not a clean one. The Quiet Revolution was only the first phase of a long process of transformation. Over the last 30 years nationalists have struggled with the tensions between the old and the new forms. As a result, nationalist thought has moved progressively away from *la survivance* and toward a more secular and liberal form of nationalism.[9] How has secularization – that is, the transfer of authority from religious to secular bodies – changed Quebec nationalism?

During the Quiet Revolution, a new interest arose in using the power of the state as a means of securing and promoting the interests of "the nation." On the one hand, this led nationalists to reflect more carefully on the relationship between their nationalist objectives and their commitment to respect individual freedom and equality. As a result, nationalism post-1960s has become progressively more liberal in outlook. This has reached a point where, at the level of Quebec's internal politics, most nationalists now hold a view of "the nation" that is quite different from that of their spiritual fathers (see below). Thus far, they are all "new" nationalists.

However, when the discussion shifts to the question of Quebec's place in Confederation, many are still tempted by a strain of nationalism rooted in *la survivance.* That is, they cling to the old view of "the nation" which, like Allaire's view of culture, comprises almost everything. This has created a serious problem. For, unlike the old nationalists of the pre-1960 period, those who approach federalism in this way today view the state as the principal tool for the promotion of the unique identity and interests of "the nation." They are thus led, like Allaire, to the conclusion that the National Assembly "needs" control over a wide range of powers (or independence) in order adequately to protect and promote the community's special interests.

If contemporary Quebec nationalism has, in one form, reached a point where it is no longer compatible with federalism, it is because it combines vestiges of the old doctrine of *la survivance* with the new activist vision of the state that arose in the 1960s. From the point of view of federalism, this hybrid of the old and new nationalisms is unworkable. Its demands for control over the power of the state have no principled limits and hence are insatiable. In our view, an accommodation between nationalism and federalism is possible only if nationalists accept that the objective of using the state to promote the special interests of "the nation" must be disciplined by (relatively) well-defined conceptions of "the nation," "identity" and "culture." If the pre-1960s nationalists had managed to accommodate with federalism a robust conception of the meanings of these terms, it is precisely because they had not linked the promotion of these interests so clearly with state activism.

THREE PROBLEMS IN CONTEMPORARY NATIONALIST THOUGHT

The internal transformation of nationalist thought has been greatly influenced by an ongoing engagement of three key questions:

(1) How is "the nation" to be defined?
(2) What is the place of the immigrant community in Quebec?
(3) What is the place of the anglophone minority in Quebec?

Defining "the Nation"

The idea of *la survivance* was essentially that nationalism is the expression of the will of a people to survive – that is, to preserve its language and culture (especially religion). This might seem to imply that "the nation" includes all who share the common language and history. In fact, the issue has raised controversy since at least the early part of this century.

In the 1920s and 1930s, nationalist thought passed through a "provincialist" phase in which it became narrowly focussed on Quebec, with some even advocating separation. One consequence of the explicit link between territory and the concept of "the nation" was that a cleavage opened up between French-speaking Canadians inside and outside Quebec. Intellectuals such as Henri Bourassa who defended the view that French Canadians were a single nation began to appear the exception rather than the rule.[10] Nonetheless, two things ensured that the sense of solidarity remained strong. First, the emphasis that *la survivance* placed on preserving language and culture (especially religion) meant there was still much common ground between Quebec nationalists and francophones outside of Quebec.

Second, as already noted, nationalists had not yet appreciated the importance of the state as a means for achieving certain ends. The tight link that now exists between the pursuit of nationalist goals and control over state institutions was far weaker in the 1920s and 1930s. Influenced by the clergy (and their doctrine of *la survivance*), nationalists of the day were at best cool to the idea of state intervention to promote economic or social goals. By the early 1940s, André Laurendeau had turned the tide somewhat and attracted support for some economic reforms, but the plan was eventually abandoned. As for the idea of greater state involvement in education, health or welfare, nationalists remained openly hostile to it.[11]

By 1960, however, the defeat of the *Union nationale* and the waning influence of the Church had paved the way for a new relationship between nationalism and the state. Under the Lesage government a new and energetic generation of Quebec nationalists put the growing bureaucracy to work in the service of "the nation." Their vision of Confederation as a pact between two nations, their goal of making Quebecers "masters in their own house" and their conviction that state intervention was the key to achieving that end – all pointed in the direction of greater state activism and greater provincial autonomy. Thus, a new relationship between nationalism and the state was forged, and the latter (symbolized by the National Assembly) emerged as the vehicle of choice for the expression and promotion of nationalist objectives.

One consequence of the new relationship and the new activism was that French-Canadian nationalism became virtually identified with the political aspirations of the *Québécois*. This, in turn, revived the question of how "the nation" should be defined. By insisting that Quebec was the "home" of the French Canadian people, the post-1960s nationalists had re-emphasized the territorial aspects of "the nation." In response, others, such as Pierre Trudeau, revived the counter-arguments of Henri Bourassa, replying that French Canadians constituted a single pan-Canadian community.[12]

With the rise of the *Parti québécois* in the 1970s events took a decisive turn. By making independence the over-arching objective of Quebec nationalism, *péquistes* were not only agreeing that "the nation" had a territorial aspect, they were implicitly elevating its importance above that of language and culture. "The nation" had become virtually synonymous with *les Québécois*. Certainly, *indépendantistes* must have anticipated the criticism that they were, in effect, expelling French-speaking Canadians outside Quebec from "the nation." Strategically, however, the move had a decisive advantage: it allowed the *indépendantistes* to argue that Quebecers, as a people, had a right – and a reason – to seek independence.

However, the move had further implications that the nationalists almost certainly did not anticipate. As the debate proceeded, two things became increasingly clear. One was that the secularizing trend had profoundly changed the moral parameters of nationalist thought: the new concern for individual freedom and equality imposed its own limits on the use of state power to promote the interests of "the nation." The other was that Quebec's new demographic realities were pushing the debate over "the nation" in a new direction.

The Place of the Immigrant Community

By the late 1960s two crucial facts about Quebec demography had begun to work their way into the debate over nationalism. First, widespread use of modern methods of contraception had resulted in a dramatic drop in the birth rate among francophone Quebecers. Historically among the most fertile in the industrialized world, their natality rate suddenly plummeted to one of the lowest. Second, immigration levels were rising. However, fewer immigrants were coming from the traditional sources in western Europe. Instead, many now came from countries in Asia, Africa, South America and the Caribbean, and thus were of neither French nor British ancestry (although many did come from francophone countries).

In response to the drop in the birth rate, many nationalists looked to immigration as a logical way of shoring up the numbers and reinforcing Quebec's distinctness. But the changing demographics in the immigrant population posed problems. For one thing, immigrants who spoke neither English nor French tended to integrate into the anglophone rather than francophone community. Francophone Quebecers worried that, were this trend to continue, a cumulative weakening of their demographic weight might eventually reduce them to a minority in their own province.

In fact, this problem seems to have been brought under control. The 1978 *Charte de la langue française* (Bill 101) included measures to ensure that the children of immigrants would be educated in French. While this has had serious consequences for enrolment in the anglophone school system (see below), it has also shown that relatively moderate and, we would argue, liberally acceptable forms of state regulation can effectively reverse important social trends such as these. However, a second aspect of the immigrant situation has proved more intractable. No one pretends that immigrants from nontraditional sources share francophone Quebecers' sense of history or their culture. But if they are the bulwark that is to reinforce the distinctness of Quebec society, they will have to be enlisted in the cause. In effect, they will have to become part of "the nation." Does this mean that steps will have to be taken to assimilate them to the traditions and culture of the *Québécois?*

Here the moral parameters of the new liberal trend in nationalism assert themselves. The issue of "integration" raises the thorny question of whether demanding that immigrants abandon their own culture and identity is a violation of their dignity as people. After all, it is precisely the struggle against assimilation – *la survivance* – that lies at the root of Quebec nationalism. The debate over how to integrate the immigrant community into the distinct society thus has presented nationalists with a deep dilemma. Assessing the attempt to come to grips with it takes us to the heart of the changes under way and of the tensions in Quebec nationalist thought today.

The nationalism of the pre-1960s, based on *la survivance,* aimed at preserving a quite specific cultural tradition, which was viewed as the basis of the sense of community within "the nation." On this view, membership in "the nation" is, first and foremost, a question of ethnicity. By contrast, the new secularized nationalism of the post-1960s has come to regard some degree of cultural change and diversity as not only unavoidable but desirable. It plays down the extent to which the sense of community in "the nation" rests on common ethnic background and instead puts the emphasis on sharing a common objective: the enhancement and preservation of a thriving francophone society in the heart of North America. This is a project in which all Quebecers can participate and to which they can all contribute. The emphasis here is on the future, rather than the past; and on building something new rather than preserving something old.

This does not mean the past is unimportant. On the contrary, the existing sense of community it creates is the foundation on which the future must be built. The new nationalism puts the past in perspective. The merit of traditional practices and values is no longer taken for granted. The authority of tradition has been rejected. Change and adaptation are now seen as essential to the flourishing of "the nation." As for the source of this change, the new nationalism accepts that it can (and should) come from "outside" (e.g., from immigrants) as well as from "inside" (i.e., "old stock" or *Québécois pure laine*) "the nation." In these respects, the new nationalism is, relatively speaking, confident, outward looking and liberal while the old nationalism is defensive, inward looking and conservative.[13]

Anglophones in Quebec

The restrictions on education, commercial signs and the use of English in the workplace contained in Bill 101 provoked a clash between nationalists and the anglophone minority over the nature of individual freedom and equality in a liberal society. Critics saw Bill 101 as an aggressive use of state power by a majority to weaken a minority and, ultimately, to coerce its members to adopt the linguistic and cultural practices of the majority. As such, they attacked Bill 101 as an affront to the values of liberty and equality on which Canada is supposed to rest. This, in turn, forced nationalists to confront and reflect on the defensive character of the old nationalism and to explain and defend its objectives, and the measures intended to promote them, in liberal terms. The debate, as we will argue below, has led to considerable evolution in nationalist thought, as well as in the nature of liberalism within the anglophone minority in Quebec, and, finally, among many English-speaking Canadians outside Quebec.

GETTING BEYOND SYMBOLISM

At the outset of this chapter we said that, while the old nationalism is not consistent with federalism, the new one is. The old one rests on a conception of Quebec's distinctness (i.e., the culture, language and identity of the *Québécois*) that is too elastic. It can be extended at will to include just about everything. We identified this elasticity as a key cause of the instability in the relationship between Quebec and the rest of Canada. On the one hand, we are convinced that a majority of francophone Quebecers believe that they share many economic, social and cultural interests with other Canadians and, as a result, are essentially federalists. On the other hand, there is a deep ambivalence over where the line is to be drawn between those things that make Quebecers distinct and those they share with other Canadians.

The 30-year debate about the "Quebec question" has been about the nature of these differences and similarities and how they should affect Quebec's place in

Confederation. At bottom, the issue seems to turn on whether a mutually acceptable understanding can be found regarding the scope and nature of Quebec's claim to distinctness. By reconceiving the basis of membership in "the nation" in terms of joint participation in the project of building a francophone society,[14] we think nationalist thought has, quite on its own, moved a considerable distance toward a more workable definition of culture.

In recent years, a growing number of Quebec nationalists have taken a clear and strong stand in favour of the new inclusive view of "the nation."[15] By so doing, they have more or less explicitly made *language* rather than ethnicity the principal tool of political and social integration. In this way, as we have seen, they have overcome the exclusionary nature of the old pre-1960s nationalism and taken a major step beyond the nationalism of *la survivance*.[16]

However, many of these same nationalists refuse to accept that the new conception of "the nation" should also define Quebec's place in Confederation. They resist the conclusion that a circumscribed definition of language, culture and identity should provide the basis for assessing Quebec's distinctness and its unique interests in Canada. On the contrary, as soon as the discussion moves from the level of Quebec's internal politics to that of Quebec's place in Canada, these nationalists revert to the logic of the old nationalism, to the elastic version of these concepts, in order to justify a radical devolution of powers or to explain the need for independence.

But the punch is gone from this sort of argument. Too often it turns into a kind of perfunctory moral imperative to the effect that "the people" should control their own destiny. Thus Rodrigue Tremblay upbraids Quebecers for their faltering will, warning them that, if they are not to lose their chance to be a real people, they must act boldly and decisively by making a fundamental political choice. According to him:

With the Charter of the French Language in 1977, the Québécois took a half-step toward the objective of controlling their political territory. It is a half-step in that, without a consolidation of Quebec control in the other vital areas of immigration, the economy, finance and general politics, this half-step could easily be reversed and result in a loss.[17]

Why, we wonder, should Bill 101 be regarded as only a "half-step?" And why should Quebecers need to seize control of "the economy, finance and general politics" before they can become a full-fledged people? As far as we can tell, "the nation" has not only survived, it is thriving.

"Arguments" of this sort reverberate with echoes of *la survivance*. Quebecers are exhorted to look on independence as a kind of test or rite of passage by which they will at last earn the badge of nationhood. This harks back to the old nationalism, with its mission of cajoling, coaxing and prodding "the nation" to keep it from languishing. In the 18th and 19th centuries – perhaps even 30 years ago – this style of argument might have had a point. Today, it sounds defensive and quaint. Among those Quebecers who are persuaded that independence is needed, we can only hope it is for better reasons than this.

For our part, we think it is time the debate moved beyond these quasi-romantic or symbolic arguments and concentrated on substance. More to the point, we think careful reflection on the changes the concept of "the nation" has undergone in nationalist thought over the last 15 years leads to the conclusion that, as far as state action is concerned, the basis of Quebec's distinctness now lies in its commitment to promote the flourishing of the French language – a job Quebecers are doing remarkably well. Moreover, the more we reflect on the changes under way in Quebec nationalist thought, the more we are convinced that there is little an independent Quebec would want to do on this front that it cannot now do. This conclusion seems to be confirmed by the reflections of some of Quebec's leading nationalist academics.

Focussing the New Nationalism: Between Symbolism and Substance

Le groupe de réflexion sur les institutions et la citoyenneté, a group of 11 academics with impeccable nationalist credentials, has called for a new "linguistic pact" in Quebec.[18] The new pact would be based on three fundamental principles that would "guide the way we approach the whole linguistic problematic in Quebec" (author's translation). The three principles are as follows:

(1) The juridical primacy of Quebec in linguistic matters.
(2) The affirmation of the French language as the principal language of Quebec.
(3) The recognition that English and certain Aboriginal languages have a special historical status and form part of the heritage of Quebec.

Let us say a few words about each principle, beginning with the last.

We must set aside the question of the status of the eight Aboriginal languages in Quebec. The complexities involved demand a far more detailed discussion than could be given here. In the last chapter we acknowledged the historical importance of First Nations' languages. Suffice it to say that we agree that some recognition of this special status is appropriate.

As for the place of English in Quebec, what strikes us, both in the proposal for a new pact and the present state of the language debate in Quebec, is the extent to which the two sides – anglophone and francophone – have moved toward a common centre.[19] On the one hand, most young anglophones in Quebec are now bilingual,[20] accept French as the language of the workplace in Quebec and generally agree that the children of immigrants should be schooled in French. On the other hand, we are convinced that most Quebec nationalists genuinely want the anglophone community in that province to flourish. Increasingly, it is recognized that mastery of English is crucial to the province's success in the global economy. The anglophone community is seen as making a vital contribution to Quebec's financial, institutional and human capital, as well as to the cultural richness of Quebec.

From the point of view of Quebec anglophones, the two main areas of concern in recent years seem to be the drop in enrolment in their schools and restrictions on the use of English on signs.[21] The latter were confirmed by the Bourassa government in 1988 in Bill 178.[22] They have since been eased considerably under the Liberal government's Bill 86, passed in the spring of 1993. We will not revisit the debate on the sign law. We note only that in their document the authors of the proposal for a new pact explicitly call for a repeal of the 1988 ban on bilingual signs. Suffice it to say that its proclamation in 1988 was followed by a tidal wave of anger among Quebec anglophones and English-speaking Canadians outside Quebec, as well as criticism from the international community. Since then there has been increasing unease among nationalists about the use of such measures. We take this as strong evidence that the liberalizing trend of the new nationalism has made nationalists increasingly conscious of the need to square their objectives with widely established liberal norms on the respect for individual equality and freedom.

On the issue of the present state of anglophone schools, we note that almost no one in that community is calling for a return to the pre-Bill 101 days when immigrants were free to send their children to English schools. Without underestimating the differences of opinion that still exist on various aspects of the language question, or the gravity of the problem in the anglophone school system, we must say that we are struck by the fact that relations between the two principal linguistic communities in Quebec have improved substantially in the last decade and that, as far as we can tell, the issues on which attention is now focussed do not seem to rest on deep and irreconcilable philosophical differences over the role of government in a liberal society.

Regarding the second principle suggested by the authors of the new pact (the affirmation of French as the principal language of Quebec), we take it from their document that the principle aims at promoting two main objectives: that French remain the principal language of the workplace and government; and that French be the language in which the children of immigrants are educated. Our main concern here is that adequate provisions be in place to ensure the continued flourishing of the anglophone community – a point on which the authors of the proposal themselves insist. Let us, then, underline here our own support for what we see as the basic principle of the new nationalism, namely, that membership in "the nation" is defined by participation in the development of a flourishing francophone society in the heart of North America. If Quebecers are to achieve this goal, we take it as axiomatic that French will be the principal language of that society.

As for the remaining principle – affirmation of the juridical primacy of Quebec in linguistic matters – it leaves us perplexed and concerned. Not because we wish, reflexively, to oppose it. Rather, because we find ourselves wondering what, exactly, is at issue. Nor is the document very helpful in this regard. On the one hand, the authors make a point of declaring, with a carefully crafted mix of defiance and solemnity, that, if necessary, the Quebec government should not hesitate to invoke the "notwithstanding clause" in the Charter of Rights; that is, it should not hesitate to pass language legislation aimed at ensuring the promotion of Quebec's legitimate language interests, even if it contravenes the Charter.[23] The authors are, we note, careful to add immediately that any such measures must not violate liberal or international norms. Oddly, they give no specific examples of measures that might actually fit into this apparently critical, yet remarkably vague, category.

Now it may well be that examples of such measures exist; and that nationalists would largely agree that their implementation is crucial to realizing the goal of a thriving francophone society. But if the meta-vision we have been arguing for throughout this book were accepted, we think such measures might well be success-fully defended against a Charter challenge precisely because they are both liberal and crucial to the development and preservation of a flourishing Quebec society. As such, we would argue that, under section 1 of the Charter, they constitute a "reason-able limit" on individual rights in the province of Quebec.

Secondly, the very fact that the authors' discussion of this principle revolves around hypothetical rather than actual issues seems to us telling evidence about how much the gap between nationalists and federalists in Quebec has narrowed. When Bill 101 was passed in 1978, no one needed to muse about hypothetical pos-sibilities. The debate was over two radically different visions of the role of the state in a liberal society – visions that had given rise to concrete policies, not just intel-lectual anxieties over theoretical differences that, one day, might show up in policy. Clearly, the climate has changed.

This leaves us wondering what the authors of the proposal for a new pact really think is at issue when they insist that the National Assembly must make a "solemn declaration" of its juridical primacy in matters of language. In the absence of any specific examples to analyze or debate, it is hard to see what real substantial issues this principle is meant to address. Even at the abstract level of constitutional theory, such a "declaration" serves no point for it would have absolutely no legal force or significance.[24]

Perhaps what the authors have in mind is something that would provide the con-stitutional recognition of the unique place of Quebec in the Canadian federation. This "principle" was enunciated as the fundamental concern in Quebec's "five points" of 1986, which led to the Meech Lake Accord.[25] If so, why not wait for a more opportune moment when that issue can be dealt with directly, say, through a constitutional amendment, rather than inciting the Quebec government to undertake acts or gestures that have no constitutional significance and will only create contro-versy and uncertainty about its intentions?

We are aware that constitutional recognition of this sort would be more than pure symbolism, even if it were accompanied, as in the Meech Lake Accord, by a clear statement that the recognition of distinctness did not confer new legislative powers on the province of Quebec. The recognition would still be a constitutional fact that would have to be weighed in judicial interpretation whenever it was relevant to a particular issue. That is something very different from a new power, but it would ensure that Quebec's distinctness was not overlooked. We supported the constitutional recognition of Quebec's distinctness in the past and continue to do so today.

Apart from the uncertainty associated with this principle, the substantive views expressed in the authors' document appear to us quite moderate and their goals generally consistent with the vision of federalism we defend in this book. We therefore see nothing in what they say that necessitates independence – or even a major devolution of powers. The moderateness of their position is, we think, a reflection of the fact that, symbolism aside, they agree with the principle on which the new nationalism rests. Now, suppose they were to go one step further and agree with us that the new definition of "the nation" – and, for the purposes of public policy, the identification of culture with language it implies – should not be confined to internal discussions of the nature of Quebec's special cultural interests, but also should be extended to the external sphere, that is, to debates over Quebec's place in Confederation. What consequences would this shift in outlook have for nationalists' traditional claims that Quebec needs more control over powers or that independence is the best way to promote the interests of "the nation?"

The new nationalism not only limits the kinds of measures nationalists can implement within Quebec to promote integration and national identity. It also implicitly limits the scope of the arguments they can fairly make in the federal context in the name of the National Assembly's responsibility to "preserve and promote" Quebec's special interests. Consider the following example.

In the 1970s and early 1980s the *Caisse de dépôt* used the funds accumulated under the Quebec Pension Plan to subsidize Quebec industry in a variety of ways. The goal was to foster a strong Quebec business sector owned by Quebecers as well as to develop a new class of francophone managers and business people. The plan was remarkably successful on both fronts. As a result, some have argued that the kind of government-business partnership that was established is an integral part of Quebec as a "distinct society."

Perhaps this is so. But, on our interpretation of the distinct society, not much follows from it. While it may be plausible to argue that certain forms of commercial regulation or subsidy are needed to ensure the use of French in the workplace – an objective that clearly is an integral part of the "national project"[26] – the claim that the financial practices of the *Caisse* are "cultural" seems suspiciously like special pleading.

A full economic union allows for the free flow of goods, services, labour and capital. Implicit in this is the idea that equal treatment should be given to all businesses, regardless of their place of origin. If a business based in Alberta seeks to set up operations in Quebec, it should receive the same treatment from the Quebec government (and its agencies) as would a local business. Quebec nationalists cannot reasonably expect the rest of Canada to except from the "equal treatment" rule the *Caisse*'s preferential financing policies toward Quebec businesses, on the grounds that its role in maintaining a special government-business partnership is crucial to promoting Quebec's "cultural distinctness." From the point of view of public policy, this stretches too far the concept of "cultural distinctness." Such arguments should carry little if any weight in, say, discussions over the elimination of interprovincial trade barriers.

This is not simply to deny the validity of developing government-business partnerships. How much room the Constitution, or an internal trade agreement, ought to leave to provincial governments to engage in strategic economic development is a question for debate. But when the Quebec government sits down with other governments to discuss the issue, it should not expect special treatment on the grounds that Quebec is a distinct society. If it wishes to insist on the need to protect, say, the practices of the *Caisse*, these should be seen for what they are: regional economic development policies. As such, they are part of a cluster of issues and problems that concern all Canadians, not just Quebecers. Any concessions made to Quebec on this front would thus have to be offset by parallel concessions to the other provinces.[27]

But what, exactly, does this mean for nationalists who favour either independence or a major devolution of powers to Quebec? At least two things. First, arguments exhorting Quebecers to opt for independence in order to preserve or promote their distinctive cultural-linguistic interests, or as a way of fulfilling their destiny as a sovereign people, simply misconstrue the nature of French-speaking Quebecers' special interests. As the full implications of the new nationalists' definition of "the nation" are digested, it becomes more and more difficult to see why many claims still advanced in its name should be viewed as having any significant connection with promoting national identity. Second, as this becomes clearer, the weakness of appeals to nationalism as a basis for seeking independence or a major devolution of powers will also become apparent. In response, some will search for new arguments to justify their longstanding demands for new powers or their commitment to independence.

An obvious strategy is to focus on practical concerns over economic and administrative efficiency, and to argue that "federalism just is not working."[28]

Regarding this second point, let us agree that strong arguments exist for seeking a rearrangement of some roles and responsibilities in the federation, particularly in areas such as labour market training and immigration. Given the extent to which globalization and freer trade are restructuring the Canadian economy and redefining the nature of work, it would be an almost miraculous coincidence if the *status quo* turned out to be the optimal arrangement. But, as we will argue in the next chapter, while reorganization is needed, much of this can begin through nonconstitutional methods such as administrative agreements. These agreements can be far more nuanced, and are more easily amended to take account of changing circumstances, than would be a series of changes to the division of powers. Such arrangements may well lead to constitutional reform, though probably not in the immediate future.

Conclusion

If one asks a conventional political theorist why Quebecers tend to embrace concepts such as "sovereignty-association" or "cultural sovereignty," often the answer is that they want to have their cake and eat it too. We think the ambivalence of the terms points to something important. It suggests that the *Québécois* not only distinguish their cultural-linguistic interests from other interests but that they are concerned to find a good balance between the promotion of their different interests.

In particular, many *Québécois* feel an ambivalence toward Canada that suggests their attachment to it goes beyond mere economic interest. While federalists in Quebec often defend federalism in terms of the economic benefits it brings to their province, we believe many *Québécois* still share the sense of community that underwrites the Canadian social and political union. The challenge is to define the different interests so that a workable balance can be struck between the promotion of national identity, a sense of membership in the Canadian political community and mutual economic interests.

If the shifts in Quebec nationalist thought traced in this chapter are right, for new nationalists, membership in "the nation" is based on a common commitment among citizens to the goal of maintaining Quebec as a flourishing francophone society in the heart of North America. Language is the principal tool for promoting this special goal. This vision of Quebec is consistent with the meta-vision for Canadian federalism developed in this book. However, in closing, we want to clarify two points about the views expressed in the chapter.

First, we have not argued that Quebec's distinctness is "just a matter of language." Our argument is that, insofar as the National Assembly has a special mission in Confederation, measures to fulfil that mission should focus on language. Our equation of language and culture is "methodological," not "sociological." Sociologically, we agree that living in Quebec is a unique cultural experience that goes far beyond the spoken word. But methodologically, we need a way to put reasonable limits on the range of policy issues where the National Assembly can legitimately claim a special right to act in the interests of "the nation." We think the French language is the key policy tool for promoting and maintaining the distinct society. The National Assembly therefore sometimes may need to make special claims on its citizens, the federal government or the courts to ensure the flourishing of the language and the realization of the Assembly's mission. Thus it may be that constitutional recognition of this mission, some special regulatory measures, federal-provincial administrative arrangements or applications of the Charter will be justified in the area of language policy.

Second, we are not ruling out that other arrangements or changes may be needed to meet Quebec's needs. But if measures unrelated to language are proposed, they should be presented, discussed and assessed in terms of some aspect of Quebec's particular needs as a *regional* community in the federation, not as a cultural or linguistic one. These might involve concerns about efficiency, democratic accountability or regional economic development. None, however, is directly linked to the National Assembly's special mission in Confederation. Rather, they are concerns shared by governments and citizens across the country.

As for the independence option, we simply do not see how, at this juncture in history, a dramatic political rupture with Canada will help Quebecers solve their economic and social problems. The economic interdependence of Quebec and the rest of Canada (especially Ontario) is now so great that opting for independence, far from simplifying the situation, would almost certainly compound the difficulties, as governments tied themselves in knots trying to negotiate Canada's deconstruction. With the massive changes now under way at the global level, we think Canadians ought to be working on a policy of strategic cooperation, rather than internal division, to find ways to further their common interests in a very competitive world.

Notes

1. *The Globe and Mail*, March 3, 1994, p. A1.

2. Alain Dubuc, "The new Quebec nationalism," *The Network*, Vol. 2, nos. 6-7 (June-July 1992), pp. 14-15.

3. During the Canada Round, former Quebec Premier Robert Bourassa proved to be a master of this ambiguity in Quebec politics. No one was sure exactly where on the spectrum he stood.

4. Jean Allaire, "The Allaire Report and the federal proposals: a comparison," *The Network*, Vol. 1, no. 5 (October 1991), p. 10.

5. Allaire, "A comparison," p. 10.

6. Kenneth McRoberts and Dale Posgate, *Quebec: Social Change and Political Crisis*, 2nd. ed. (Toronto: McClelland and Stewart, 1984), p. 33.

7. Counter-currents existed. Henri Bourassa's vision of a bicultural Canada was in important respects anti-provincialist; and André Laurendeau's efforts to develop a socially progressive nationalism were liberal in outlook. See Michael Oliver, *The Passionate Debate: The Social and Political Ideas of Quebec Nationalism 1920-45* (Montreal: Véhicule Press, 1991), chap. 5.

8. These reforms included the nationalization of *Hydro Québec*, the creation of the *Société générale de financement* and the *Caisse de dépôt et placement du Québec*, as well as reforms in social policy and culture.

9. Some will regard the idea of "liberal nationalism" as an oxymoron. As should be evident from our chapter 5, we do not. Indeed, in recent years there has been considerable discussion of liberal nationalism among liberals. Recent books on the subject include Yael Tamir, *Liberal Nationalism* (Princeton: Princeton University Press, 1993); and Will Kymlicka, *Liberalism, Community and Culture* (Oxford: Clarendon Press, 1989).

10. See Oliver, *The Passionate Debate*, p. 148. Elsewhere Oliver notes: "In a letter replying to a compatriot who suggested the separatist solution, Bourassa specifically rejected the idea, on the grounds of constitutional and geographic difficulties, and because it would mean the abandonment of French Canadian groups in other provinces" (p. 29).

11. See McRoberts and Posgate, *Quebec: Social Change and Political Crisis*, p. 67.

12. Pierre Elliott Trudeau, "Quebec and the Constitutional Problem," in *Federalism and the French Canadians* (Toronto: Macmillan Company, 1968), p. 30.

13. For a discussion of the shift in nationalist thought toward the new model of "the nation," see Louis Balthazar, "Entrevue avec Louis Balthazar," in Gilles Gougeon (ed.), *Histoire du nationalisme Québécois: Entrevues avec sept spécialistes* (Montréal: vlb éditeur, 1994), pp. 159-70.

14. There is, of course, also a territorial criterion: to be a member of "the nation" one must reside in Quebec. Oddly, many nationalists talk as though this were the only thing that counted (see, for example, note 16 below). This is surely an exaggerated claim and a view no nationalist really holds. One need only scan the debates over language and immigration to see that language is central to all nationalists' vision of Quebec as a society and of Quebecers as a nation.

15. A few examples are Lise Bissonnette, Christian Dufour, Alain Dubuc, Guy Laforest, José Woehrling, Daniel Turp, Alain Noël and Josée Legault.

16. As Lucien Bouchard puts it: "Our nationalism is not that of the 1930s, it is not based upon ethnicity, it is based upon territory and it states that all people who live in Quebec are equal and that democracy will be the reality in all circumstances" (author's translation), "Une victoire de Johnson remettrait en cause l'existence du Bloc," *Le Devoir*, March 25, 1994.

17. Author's translation, *Le Devoir*, June 30, 1993.

18. They are Claude Bariteau, Guy Laforest, Gary Caldwell, Yolande Cohen, Alain-G. Gagnon, Daniel Latouche, Alain Noël, Pierre-Paul Proulx, Daniel Turp, François Rocher and Daniel Salée; see *Le Devoir*, April 24-25, 1993, p. A13.

19. A remarkable example of this appeared on the op-ed page of the English-language Montreal daily *The Gazette* on June 7, 1993. Julius Grey, an outspoken defender of anglophone rights, and

Josée Legault, a passionate Quebec nationalist, jointly published an article sketching the basis of a "compromise" position on the language issue in Quebec. Perhaps Legault is not typical of Quebec nationalists. Nevertheless, that two individuals of such opposing persuasions were able to find enough common ground to reach agreement on what has been one of the most divisive issues in Quebec politics seems to us a dramatic indication that major changes are under way.

20. According to the 1991 Canadian census, 60.7 percent of Quebec anglophones are bilingual – more than double the proportion three decades ago.

21. On the crisis in the anglophone school system see the report of the Task Force on English Education, *Report to the Minister of Education of Quebec* (the Chambers Report), Gouvernement du Québec, ministère de l'Éducation (Québec: 1992).

22. Restrictions on the use of English on signs were first introduced in sections 58 and 69 of the Charter of the French Language (Bill 101) by the *Parti québécois*. However, both the Superior Court of Quebec and the Quebec Court of Appeal found the two sections to be in conflict with the Quebec Charter of Human Rights and Freedoms. This was appealed to the Supreme Court of Canada, which, in *Ford v. Quebec (AG)* ([1988] 2 S.C.R. 712), upheld the ruling and noted that the sections were also in conflict with section 2(b) of the Canadian Charter of Rights and Freedoms. Bill 178 was introduced subsequently by the Bourassa government. The notwithstanding clause was invoked to ensure the restrictions would not be struck down under the Canadian Charter.

23. The notwithstanding clause, section 33 of the Charter, can be invoked by governments to pass legislation to exempt a particular law from key sections of the Charter. Such legislation must be renewed every five years. Bill 178, the law passed by the Bourassa government in 1988 preventing the use of English on outdoor commercial signs, relied on the use of this clause.

24. This point is brought out nicely by Josée Legault and Julius Grey in a commentary on the proposal for a new pact. See "Pacte ou compromis linguistique?", *Le Devoir*, May 11, 1993.

25. See David Milne, *The Canadian Constitution* (Toronto: James Lorimer and Company, 1991), pp. 195-96.

26. See, for example, Stéphane Dion, "La langue à l'ouvrage," *Le Devoir*, June 29, 1993.

27. This is a rule of thumb, not an absolute principle. There may be exceptions. For instance, data released by Statistics Canada suggest that, in the two decades since the federal government committed itself to improving the economic position of francophones, the income gap between francophones and anglophones has actually widened (*The Globe and Mail*, March 23, 1994). If it could reasonably be shown that: (a) a particular preferential policy of the *Caisse* aimed at, and was reasonably thought to result in, a narrowing of this gap; and (b) if there were no equally effective, non-trade distorting way of achieving the goal, a case might exist for making a special exception.

28. It is worth noting here that both the *Parti québécois* and the *Bloc québécois* have put greater emphasis on these kinds of arguments in making the case for independence and less emphasis on language and culture.

9

BETWEEN EQUALITY AND ASYMMETRY: TOWARD A MORE FUNCTIONALIST APPROACH TO THE FEDERATION

In federal systems the powers of the state are shared between the constituent governments (provinces, states, *Länder*, etc.) and the central government. The legislative arm of the central government, in turn, is composed of two assemblies: a lower house and a second chamber. These two features – the sharing of the state's powers and the bicameral structure of the central government – appear to be fundamental to the federal system of government.

Some in Canada would go further. They argue that changes to the distribution of powers or major reforms to the second chamber (the Senate) ought to conform to the principle of the equality of the provinces (PEP). In their view, the PEP should also be recognized as fundamental to the federal system. On this basis, they draw two important conclusions about Canadian federalism.

First, on the division of powers, they maintain that assigning specifically different legislative powers to Quebec – "asymmetry" – would violate the PEP and hence be unacceptable. In this chapter we consider the theoretical foundations of the PEP and assess its implications for the division of powers. We conclude that the PEP does not provide a principled basis for opposition to asymmetry. However, we go on to ask whether our system of government imposes practical limits on asymmetry as a way of responding to Quebec's longstanding demand for more powers. Our answer is that it does.

Second, on the Senate, defenders of the PEP conclude that, in addition to being elected and effective, a reformed Senate should also be equal. They contend that the PEP implies that each province should have the same number of senators. In this chapter we also ask whether the PEP can justify such a claim. We do not think that it can.

FEDERALISM AND THE EQUALITY OF THE PROVINCES

Federalism is a system intended to make the state sensitive to regional diversity in ways that do not apply in a unitary state such as France. An intervening tier of government, as in Canada, provides greater local control over decision making, as well as being a bulwark against domination by a remote national government. Thus far, most federalists would probably agree. However, some wish to go further. For example, Newfoundland Premier Clyde Wells adds an additional requirement:

> In every federation there are two essential equalities, each of which must be given a voice in the affairs of the federation. The first is the equality of each citizen, which is given a voice in the legislative chamber (in Canada, the House of Commons) elected on the basis of representation by population. The second is the equality of each constituent part, which is given a voice in a second legislative chamber (in Canada, it should be the Senate) in which there is representation from each constituent part.[1]

Wells bases two important conclusions on these views. First, "there must be a chamber of the federal legislature in which each province has an equal say in the exercise of federal legislative power."[2] Hence, he appeals to the PEP to argue for a Triple-E Senate.[3] Second, he insists that no province should have a "special status," in the sense that it exercises constitutional powers or rights not available to the others.[4] During the Canada Round, Wells thus appealed to the PEP as a reason for objecting to proposals for an asymmetrical arrangement of powers for Quebec. Why does Wells believe all provinces are equal? He explains his views this way: "Equality is derived from the right to participate on an equal basis with the other provinces..."[5]

With respect, this is hardly illuminating. Premier Wells is, of course, right to insist that, if provinces have a right to participate on an equal basis, then their equality can be derived from that right. But that is only to say that, if there is a provincial right to equal participation, then provinces are equal with respect to that right – which is neither controversial nor informative. Indeed, it only begs the harder questions: *Do* provinces have a right to participate on an equal basis? And, if so, *in what areas?* Does the right to participate really apply to the *exercise of federal legislative power,* as Wells claims?

To answer these questions, we need greater clarity about the origin of this "second equality." There seem to be two possible sources: comparative studies of federalism and theory. As we note further down, the idea obviously has not emerged from comparative studies. There are a number of federations – including Canada – whose second chamber is not based on this second equality. Examining different federations thus leads to the opposite conclusion, namely, that the second equality is not a fundamental feature of federations.

Presumably, then, the second equality arises from theoretical views about federalism: it is a normative concept – that is, it tells us what a "true" federation *should* look like. Those who do not conform to the norm (e.g., Canada) are deviations. What, then, is the theoretical argument for the second equality? We see only one plausible source: it is based on an analogy with the liberal principle of the equality of persons.

When Clyde Wells tells us that (a) the provinces are the "constituent parts" of the federation; and that therefore (b) they are equal to one another, we think the argument turns on a suppressed analogy. It invites us to compare provinces with individual citizens who, as the "constituent parts" of the political community, are equal to one another. The logic of the analogy then continues as follows: if democracy implies a "one person, one vote" approach to decision making among citizens, federalism implies a "one province, one vote" approach among provinces.

This analogy between provinces and citizens is not without merit. But, if this is the theoretical foundation of Premier Wells' views about the second equality, we disagree that it guarantees provinces an equal say in the exercise of federal legislative power. We also disagree with Wells' contention that the second equality rules out asymmetrical federalism.

The Analogy Between Individual and Provincial Equality

Liberalism rests on a respect for personal autonomy – that is, the capacity of citizens to make a life for themselves by choosing who and what they want to be. It is in terms of their right to exercise this capacity for self-definition that they are all equal. And it is out of respect for this capacity – "human dignity" – that the state affirms and guarantees rights.

How might this view of liberal equality be applied to provinces in a federal system? An analogy between the equality of individuals and that of provinces would have to turn on the claim that both provinces and people have a capacity for autonomy, and hence an equal right to exercise it freely by making decisions about the promotion of their own integrity, goals and interests. Within the analogy, provincial governments and their legislatures would be the counterpart of the individual's capacity for choice, for these are the mechanisms by which provincial decision making occurs. If so, then to say that provinces (like individuals) are all equal would be to acknowledge that their governments and legislatures are independent and competent decision makers within their jurisdictions with an equal right to promote the integrity, goals and interests of the communities they represent.

On this reading, to say that provinces are equal is to say something about the status of their *governments and legislatures* – namely, that *each has an equal right to make decisions, policies and laws aimed at promoting the interests of the communities they represent* and so to act as an autonomous agent within the Canadian federation (subject, of course, to the other constraints set out in the Constitution).

Insofar as this analogy between citizens and provinces sheds light on widely shared intuitions about the need to respect regional diversity, it is a useful one. But does the analogy support Clyde Wells' two points about the PEP: (a) that it implies provinces should have an equal say in the exercise of federal legislative power; and (b) that it rules out asymmetrical federalism?

Two Problems with the Principle of the Equality of the Provinces

Provincial Governments *vs.* Provincial Communities

It is difficult to see how, on this analysis, provincial equality implies *anything* about provinces having a right to an equal say in the exercise of federal legislative power – say, through a Triple-E Senate. After all, what Clyde Wells and Westerners such as Preston Manning are seeking is assurance that the interests of the smaller provinces are not overshadowed. They are reacting to an uneven distribution of population which, they claim, gives Central Canada too much control over federal decision-making power.

But what does the issue of "regional fairness" have to do with the idea of provincial equality? The Senate reform debate is about how to ensure that no region of the country has too much control over the exercise of *federal* powers, not about the equal right of provinces to pursue their own interests within their own spheres of jurisdiction.

In countries that have adopted the federal system of government, the second chamber has taken different forms. Initially, in the US, for example, state governments used to appoint their representatives to the Senate. Over time, this approach fell into disrepute. US senators are now elected under popular suffrage. In Australia, members of the Senate are elected in equal number from each of the Australian states. In Germany, members of the *Bundesrat* are appointed by each state in numbers that to a limited degree reflect the size of their population. And, as we know, in Canada senators are appointed by the central government in equal number for each of four regions of the country, Ontario, Quebec, the Maritime provinces and the Western provinces.[6] Each of the two northern territories also has one representative in the Senate.

In short, it is obvious that federal countries have organized their second chambers to suit their own circumstances and needs. There is nothing in the federal experience around the world that dictates that constituent parts have a right to equal representation in the second chamber.

The distribution of legislative powers in the Constitution Act, 1867 is based upon the idea of exclusive jurisdictions. We would argue that provincial governments therefore have no more *right* to representation in a federal institution than does the federal government in a provincial one. Provincial governments are elected to exercise provincial powers, as defined by section 92 of the Constitution Act, 1867. They are now, and should continue to be, elected on the basis of policies aimed at promoting the interests associated with these powers.

If there is a rationale for providing for regional representation in federal institutions – and we think there is – it is not to protect provincial governments or promote their particular goals and objectives; it is because Canadians recognize that the exercise of federal power, and the pursuit of national objectives, can inadvertently harm regional *communities*. One simply wants to be sure that federal authorities take their interests adequately into account when defining the national interest. But it would be a serious mistake to treat a regional community's interests as identical to those of its provincial government. To do so is to collapse a crucial distinction between the different, sometimes conflicting, goals and interests of *provincial governments* and those of its citizens viewed *as members of the larger Canadian community.*

That supporters of the PEP themselves distinguish between local citizens' national interests and those of provincial governments is suggested by their general unwillingness to accept provincial delegation as a basis for senatorial selection in a reformed Senate. They have surely realized that popular election would not only confer legitimacy but also lead senators to view their task as one of ensuring that the central government's vision of the national interest adequately takes into account citizens' identification with different regional communities.

We do agree that the practice of federalism requires ongoing negotiations between governments to ensure that the federal-provincial balance, and hence provincial autonomy, is respected; and that overlap and duplication of services, and conflicts among policy objectives, are minimized. But this is *not* the same as saying that it is of the essence of federalism that provincial governments should have a say in the exercise of federal legislative power or that provinces have a right to equal representation in the Senate.

But if the PEP does not support the claim that provinces have a right to equal representation in federal institutions, what about the claim that all provinces should have the same rights and powers? This brings us to the second of Clyde Wells' points: his opposition to asymmetry.

Sameness of Treatment *vs.* Substantive Equality

The idea that equality requires sameness of treatment rests on what is often called formal equality. This is certainly an important part of what constitutes liberal equality. But it is not enough. Formal equality fails to take into account the very different *consequences* that sameness of treatment may have for different individuals.

To treat two people equally, sometimes we need to know something about their particular needs and circumstances. Generally speaking, Canadians accept that for everyone to have a fair chance at a full life it is not enough simply to treat them the same way with respect to their abstract capacities as persons. We must also aim at some kind of rough equality with respect to their actual circumstances, insofar as these bear on their ability to exercise their capacity for freedom. Sometimes this means treating people *differently* in order to ensure equality.

The claim that provincial equality implies sameness of treatment is open to the same kind of objection raised against a formal approach to the equality of persons. Those who argue this way seem to confuse the (sound) claim that the federal government should treat the interests of all provinces with equal concern and respect with the (unsound) claim that all provinces should be treated the same. This ignores the fact that provinces (like individuals) sometimes have special needs or may be burdened by circumstances.

Thus, for example, unemployment insurance benefits may differ from region to region depending on the local rate of unemployment. Current federal programs to support and retrain fishermen in Newfoundland are a response to special regional circumstances and needs. Western grain transportation subsidies answer the needs of Prairie farmers. Quebec and First Nations, we have argued, have unique needs and interests with respect to language and culture.[7] But, ironically, on Clyde Wells' logic, the fact that these needs are unique becomes a reason to prevent the federal state from adjusting to respond to them. This seems to us to fly in the face of the fundamental reason for the commitment to federalism – respect for diversity.

If there is a theoretical sense in which provinces are all equal, it has to do with the right of their legislatures to promote the provincial community's interests without undue interference from the federal government. But this is essentially what we mean by the respect for regional diversity. Those who object to asymmetry on the ground that it violates the PEP mistakenly believe that the principle precludes federalism from recognizing, or providing for, substantive differences among provinces.

Asymmetry: An Answer to the Quebec Question?

For 30 years Canadians have debated whether devolving powers from the federal to provincial governments as a way of meeting Quebec's longstanding demand for greater autonomy would result in a country that is too decentralized. While some in English-speaking Canada —particularly in Alberta and British Columbia – have shown openness to greater decentralization after the Meech Lake and Charlottetown rounds, it seems fair to say that Quebecers' aspirations for more powers go beyond what most in the rest of Canada are ready to accept by way of general decentralization of federal powers. As a result, some commentators in English-speaking Canada now argue that the answer to the Quebec question lies in constitutional asymmetry.[8]

Of course, some constitutional asymmetry already exists. Under section 129 of the Constitution Act, 1867, for example, Quebec's right to use a distinctive legal system – the Civil Code – was preserved. Similarly, under section 93(2) certain education rights were guaranteed for religious minorities in Ontario and Quebec. And there are other examples.[9] However, as a strategy to accommodate Quebec, constitutional asymmetry, in the sense of specifically different powers for Quebec, has hit a roadblock. Opposition to it in English-speaking Canada, especially the West, has been fierce – much of it supported by a view of the PEP similar to that defended by Clyde Wells.

In reply, some advocates of asymmetry now propose what one commentator has called "*quid pro quo* asymmetry."[10] Philip Resnick, a supporter of this approach, describes it this way: "For every transfer of power to Quebec, there must be a corresponding reduction in the power of MPs, ministers and civil servants from Quebec where the rest of Canada is concerned."[11] Thus, in exchange for exclusive control over a significant number of new powers, Quebec's MPs would no longer vote on matters in these areas raised in the House of Commons. But, as Resnick notes, this option might require the development of something like what he calls a "Monday-Wednesday-Friday" style of governance. In his scenario, three days of the week, Quebec MPs would meet with the rest of the House to debate and vote on common matters. Two days a week, only Members from the rest of Canada would meet. In effect, there would be two Houses of Commons, and quite possibly two Cabinets.[12]

Even though we have argued that, in principle, there is nothing wrong with constitutional asymmetry, we object to arrangements that would bring about these kinds of results. In our view, they would only make Parliament unworkable, with the result that the whole country would suffer.

Moreover, any attempt to come to grips with Quebec's demand for more powers must be sensitive to the ever-increasing interdependence of federal and provincial governments in modern Canada. A *quid pro quo* arrangement such as Resnick's fails this test. On the contrary, it distracts attention from the challenges posed by interdependence and, as such, may prevent the emergence of much-needed reforms in the way Canadians practice federalism.

The Interdependence of Federal and Provincial Governments

When drafting the British North America Act, the Fathers of Confederation apparently thought those interests that had given rise to the concern over diversity were (more or less) local, identifiable and separable from those that citizens of the new state would hold in common. They drafted a division of legislative powers between Parliament and the legislatures that in their view adequately reflected this division of interests. Each of the two orders of government would be generally sovereign in its own sphere. This is classical federalism, based on a distinction between a "national" interest (to be promoted by the federal government) and a more "local" or regional one (to be promoted by provincial and local governments).

In 1867, when the Fathers of Confederation laid the foundation of Canadian federalism, the role of government was far more limited than now. As was pointed out by the *Report of the Special Joint Committee on a Renewed Canada:*

> Governments were primarily responsible for providing a legal framework within which society could go about its daily business, for providing a limited number of services, such as law enforcement, national defence, roads, bridges, and for supporting major public works such as canals and railways. Government spending was small and only of limited use as a policy tool.[13]

Matters considered to be interprovincial or international, or indeed national, in scope would be assigned to Parliament. These included interprovincial and international trade, customs, the postal service, navigation and shipping, banking and the issue of money, weights and measures, criminal law, patents and copyrights. In the provincial domain were placed all matters of a "local or private nature," including property and civil rights, lands belonging to the province, hospitals, municipal institutions, local works and education.

In those days, these were the matters considered deserving of government attention and action. With hindsight, we can see that the lists reflect a quite limited view of the role of government. Since that time, however, the role of government has undergone considerable change.

By the end of the Second World War governments across the western world had adopted a far more activist approach to governance. They had come to see themselves as having key roles in the economy, as well as in promoting the social and cultural well-being of their citizens. In Canada, this raised a particular problem. Many of the areas of jurisdiction granted to the provinces by the British North America Act – e.g., health and education – turned out to be the most costly to maintain. Yet the Act had given the major levers of taxation to the federal government.

The problem was solved through the development of a series of programs in which both governments share the expense. Initially in these arrangements, the federal government paid part of the cost of a program in an area of exclusive provincial jurisdiction. In exchange, the provinces were usually required to meet certain objectives, conditions or standards set out by the federal government. Since 1977 conditions have been removed from much of the money transferred to the provinces. Today they remain attached mainly to two programs: the Canada Assistance Plan, which helps fund social assistance, and funding for health care.

At the same time, the federal government, independently from the provinces, and using its spending power, established programs in many areas considered to be the exclusive legislative jurisdiction of the provinces, such as housing, forestry, mining, recreation and municipal affairs.

The emergence of the federal "spending power" as a key instrument in the practice of modern federalism reflects the changes in Canadian society and indeed in the approach to governance since 1867. As such, it underlies the fact that the matters over which governments have legislative jurisdiction in sections 91 and 92 of the Constitution Act, 1867 are an inadequate guide to the roles and responsibilities of government in Canada today.[14] What appeared in 1867 to be a relatively tight compartmentalization of government roles and responsibilities has since become a complex web of policy fields, entangling federal and provincial governments. Despite the apparent rigidity and obsolescence of the division of legislative powers, the spending power is the instrument that has allowed the federal government to ensure all Canadians benefit from certain basic services and opportunities.

Most provinces, led by Quebec, have traditionally resented federal "intrusion" into their jurisdictions through its use of the spending power. Clearly, there is some just ground for the provinces' resentment over the impact that the uncontrolled use of the federal spending power has had on their autonomy – especially where this involved unilateral federal decision making about joint programs.

The reality, however, is that without the federal spending power the country could not have grown and developed as it has. Canadian society is defined by its commitment to such over-arching goals and values as the respect for regional and cultural diversity, the promotion of social justice and individual freedom and the establishment of equality of opportunity. Promoting these requires both a respect for provincial autonomy and a meaningful federal presence in most policy fields. Unfortunately, the two are often in tension, if not open conflict. What is required, surely, is not the complete elimination of the spending power but a better understanding (or definition) of the circumstances under which federal spending in areas of exclusive provincial legislative jurisdictions would be appropriate.

This is a critical point, as this tension is perhaps the defining feature of modern federalism. Recognizing its importance, most observers have abandoned the classical view that roles and responsibilities can be adequately assigned, once and for all, by means of a list dividing the matters over which each order of government would have exclusive legislative authority. Instead, federalism is now seen as a dynamic system in which a constant balance must be struck between two different, and often competing, sets of social and political forces: the centralizing ones of national integration; and the decentralizing ones of provincial or local autonomy. Federalism, in short, is now viewed as more than a *structure;* it is also a *process.* As such, the act of federating is never complete. It is always a work in progress.[15]

Taking this perspective underlines the importance of maintaining a workable federal-provincial balance. But it also shifts attention away from the classical approach of making constitutional powers the principal guide to defining roles and responsibilities. Let us briefly consider what would happen if we tried to take the classical approach to defining roles and responsibilities in a policy field such as the environment.

The federal government now has exclusive jurisdiction in fisheries, criminal law, navigation and shipping, international and interprovincial rivers, coastal waters, international and interprovincial transportation, industrial activity in sectors under federal control (such as atomic energy) and federal public lands. It also has extensive taxation and emergency powers. All these have important environmental aspects. Provincial governments have control over municipalities (and hence local zoning and the disposal of sewage, garbage and waste), licensing of businesses and industries (and hence their disposal and manufacturing practices), provincial lands (and hence forestry and mining), as well as a wide range of other responsibilities falling under the category of property and civil rights. All these areas have important environmental aspects.

These two lists are not exhaustive. Still, a glance should make it obvious that neither order of government could divest itself of its environmental responsibilities. These are intricately woven into both governments' day-to-day activities through all sorts of regulatory regimes, licensing standards, programs and policies in a host of areas. To instruct either level of government to purge itself of all environmentally related interests and activities would be like telling a logger to cut only the brown parts of the tree and to leave untouched anything green.

These days, attempts to classify particular policy fields such as the environment, consumer protection, social services, regional development, labour market training, transport or culture as falling, for all governmental purposes, within the exclusive domain of either order of government are not sustainable. Both orders have responsibilities for some aspects of these policy fields. The exercise of these responsibilities requires that both governments enact laws, establish programs and use their taxing and spending authorities.

Emphasizing the Flexibility in Federalism

As a result of the many changes since 1867, including new views of government's role in society, the Constitution may need revisions. However, we doubt that the best way to proceed is to establish a new division of powers. For the reasons just given, it seems to us very unlikely that, in the end, this would constitute a marked improvement over the current division of powers.

In reality, the pace of change, the intensity of market competition and the sheer breadth of governments' involvement in day-to-day activities make the need for adjustment to the federal-provincial balance constant and ongoing. These facts argue strongly against using narrowly and rigidly defined subject matters as a way of regulating the federal-provincial balance.

As governments, both federal and provincial, pause to redefine their roles and responsibilities across the spectrum of their activities – including their relations with each other – they must be urged to develop a more "functionalist" approach to federalism. In other words, governments should place the emphasis on defining roles and responsibilities by reference to specific objectives rather than exclusive jurisdictions.

In many fields, the principle of subsidiarity may be helpful. This principle, cited in the Single European Act that established the European Community (now called the European Union, or EU), reflects the view that decision making should remain at the "lowest" government level (in the case of the EU, the national one) unless moving it up a level (i.e., to the Union) would lead to important efficiency gains. The preference for leaving decision making at the "lower" levels reflects the view that the closer decision making is to the people affected, the more democratic and responsive it is likely to be. The existing arrangement between the federal and Quebec governments in the area of immigration provides an example of how subsidiarity can lead to a more functional distribution of roles and responsibilities.

Unlike the exclusive jurisdictions in sections 91 and 92 of the Constitution, immigration is a *concurrent* jurisdiction, that is, both orders of government may legislate in the area. If there is a conflict, the laws enacted by Parliament have *paramountcy*, that is, they have precedence over those of the provinces. Under the special arrangement between Quebec and the federal government, the latter retains responsibility for what can broadly be called the "admission conditions" of immigrants. By contrast, the Quebec government has responsibility for integrating these new Canadians into the community. Thus the former decides, for example, how many immigrants will be admitted each year and from which categories, based upon an assessment of the needs of the country as a whole. The Quebec government uses its control over areas such as education, health and welfare to develop policies that will facilitate the integration of new arrivals into the local community.

The Quebec immigration agreement, therefore, reflects the subsidiarity principle and could be a model for further agreements in other areas such as labour market training, consumer protection, regional development and culture.

We do not mean to imply that the Constitution is no longer important. Nor do we think the current distribution of powers is optimal and therefore fine as it is. It would be a spectacular coincidence if the existing distribution, largely designed in 1867, were the most effective or efficient for Canada's needs in the 21st century. Nevertheless, in a modern federation such as Canada, the role that legislative categories play in maintaining a workable balance should not be exaggerated. The existing distribution of powers, while imperfect in many ways, need not prevent governments from placing more emphasis on functionalism by agreeing to assign particular responsibilities to the level of government best placed to meet them. If changes to the division of powers facilitate this, they may be desirable and should be pursued. But only after some hard questions have been asked: Which changes? Why? Are the changes essential to the discharge of the government responsibilities?

As matters stand, the best way to approach these questions may be from the bottom up. In practical terms, this means, first, that governments should examine the various policy fields, one at a time, to see what they think are Canadians' needs, both national and local. Next they should decide which order of government has the responsibility to respond to a particular need. Then each should ask whether it already has the legislative or other powers required to meet these responsibilities and the objectives to which they give rise. Only then, if a government finds that the Constitution prevents it from acting as it judges it should, would it seek a possible change to the distribution of powers in sections 91 or 92. In short, while we do not rule out the need to make changes to the Constitution, they should be contemplated only if governments hit a genuine roadblock with respect to their capacity to fulfil their particular responsibilities.

We have argued that the contemporary practice of federalism requires increased flexibility in how roles and responsibilities are allocated, and more coordination – not less – of federal-provincial policy and action. For this reason, if constitutional changes are needed, we believe that, in general, it would be better to rely on a greater use of concurrency than to create new exclusive powers – though there may well be exceptions.

Canada has made less use than most federations of concurrent jurisdictions. In 1867 the Constitution contained only two examples: agriculture and immigration. In both cases, the federal government was given paramountcy.

Section 94A, which was enacted in its current form in 1964, also provides that both Parliament and provincial legislatures may make laws in relation to old age pensions. This is the sole case where the provinces have paramountcy. In 1982, both the federal and the provincial governments were given the power to make laws concerning the export of natural resources and electrical power from a province. In this case, the federal power was made paramount.

Our reflections on the division of powers have convinced us that more emphasis on concurrency might help governments better manage some of the problems resulting from interdependence. Examples of matters where this approach might be used include broadcasting, telecommunications, interprovincial and international trade, and criminal law. In these matters the federal government would have paramountcy. Concurrency with provincial paramountcy might be desirable in labour market training, consumer protection, regional development, culture, forestry, mining, recreation, tourism, municipal affairs, housing and family policy.

A greater use of concurrent powers would allow for more flexibility in the articulation of the roles and responsibilities of each order of government and allow each province, including Quebec, to better meet its special needs.

A Mechanism for Federal-Provincial Coordination?

We have seen that, as a result of interdependence, both levels of government are now often actors in the same field. But it does not automatically follow that there is waste, overlap or duplication in the system: if each level is performing the tasks it does best, both local diversity and Canadians' common interests will be served. However, as noted, the effective coordination of objectives and action requires a joint federal-provincial effort to manage interdependence.

Interdependence hitherto has been managed on an informal basis through a host of meetings, committees, discussions and conferences ranging from simple adminis-trative matters to First Ministers meetings dealing with policy at the highest level. The informal nature of these sessions means that there are no clear rules or other criteria for decision making: each government retains responsibility for its own actions in its own field. Each must answer to its own legislature and, ultimately, its own electorate.

One consequence is that decisive action will be rare. Even when a strong majority may prefer it, agreement on policy usually is reached on the basis of the lowest common denominator – a situation that satisfies only the most reluctant party at the table. This has been especially frustrating in areas such as interprovincial trade.

In 1991 the federal government proposed measures that, in its judgement, would have strengthened the economic union and, as a result, improved governments' financial capacity to bear the increasing cost of social programs. The mechanism proposed – the Council of the Federation – would have had the power to decide on issues of intergovernmental coordination and collaboration. Decisions of the Council would have required the approval of the federal government and at least seven provinces representing 50 percent of the population.[16] The proposal received little support and was not even mentioned in the Charlottetown Accord.

The fact that this proposal was not well received does not imply that the existing unstructured and informal process is adequate for the future. We doubt, for example, this is true for economic policy and the efficient operation of the economic union. Australia, with a similar system of responsible parliamentary government, operates with a more developed Commonwealth-state structure for cooperation and decision making in economic and financial areas. This seems to have had positive effects. For example, the intergovernmental Australian Loan Council has the power to review government borrowing. It is probably not a coincidence that the level of national debt in relation to the gross domestic product is today much lower in Australia than in Canada, where no such institution exists.

More formal arrangements to manage interdependence in Canada may well be required in the future. This seems most likely for the operation of the economic union. But, as in Australia, it may also be an effective way of managing public borrowing and could also be a way of putting constraints on the use of the federal spending power. Nevertheless, Canadian governments do not now seem fully persuaded of the need for more formal arrangements. Without a real commitment at this level, we think investing time, energy and resources in the pursuit of new structures and processes would not be well spent.[17] At present, governments should concentrate their attention, in a very practical way, on the task of identifying Canadians' needs and defining the corresponding government responsibilities.

EQUALITY AND ASYMMETRY IN THE FEDERATION

We have argued that greater use of concurrent jurisdiction might help meet the concerns of Quebec in particular. Others have gone further, arguing that asymmetrical arrangements are required. Is this necessarily so?

In 1867 when the Fathers of Confederation designated agriculture and immigration as concurrent jurisdictions, it was presumably because they recognized that the interests at stake were too wide-ranging to be identified exclusively with either level of government. Doing so would have tipped the balance too far in one direction. The choice of concurrency was a way of accommodating the different but overlapping interests of the two orders of government. Over the last 30 years it has become clear that the sense of where the proper federal-provincial balance lies is different in Quebec than it is for most in the rest of the country. We have suggested that concurrency may be a way of responding to these concerns. Alternatively, in some cases the Constitution could assign to Quebec powers different from the other provinces – an asymmetrical arrangement.

The argument for asymmetry is clear: it would give greater freedom to Quebec to promote its own interests as it wishes. As well, in these same areas the rest of Canada could enjoy the advantages most provinces and people see in nationwide policies and programs. However, if asymmetry is to be accepted by a majority outside Quebec, it is likely to have to be offset by a diminished role in Parliament for Quebec – a *quid pro quo* arrangement.

We doubt this is a realistic way to respond to Quebec's aspirations. It assumes that the policy issues relating to powers devolved to Quebec could be kept separate from those relating to the powers it would share with the rest of Canada. But, if our account of interdependence is basically right, they cannot. Issues and policies in areas such as labour market training, culture, regional development, research and development and trade and industry overlap in all kinds of ways.

We fear that, in a "Monday-Wednesday-Friday" Parliament, negotiations over the classification of bills would become highly partisan. As a result, the whole process would be discredited.[18] It is also questionable whether, as proponents of asymmetry assume, most Quebecers would remain content with a Parliament where their MPs had to refrain from speaking or voting on matters of concern. And how long, we wonder, would Quebecers be willing to accept their vastly decreased influence in the federal bureaucracy?[19] In any event, if the stance we have taken in this book is right, the promotion of Quebec's special interests do not require a major devolution of legislative powers.

In principle, there is nothing wrong with asymmetry. For our part, we think some degree of it would be reasonable and legitimate, if it could be achieved without having to reconstruct Parliament. However, at least as great a role in policies and programs could probably be achieved through concurrent powers and administrative arrangements and agreements. On this approach, it also would be easier to offer the same or similar arrangements to all provinces, thereby sidestepping the question of whether or not asymmetry violates the principle of provincial equality. On the whole, then, the political and parliamentary costs of extensive constitutional asymmetry are probably too great to make it feasible. More flexibility through a greater use of concurrent powers or through intergovernmental agreements appears to us the better option.

Drawing together the main points of this and the preceding chapters, our views on the Quebec question are as follows: we do not support a new division of constitutional powers for Quebec. We do argue for clear, constitutional recognition of Quebec as a distinct society, for an interpretation of the Charter that uses section 1 to make it sensitive to Quebec's special linguistic and cultural interests and for a willingness to adopt constitutional provisions, such as concurrent powers and intergovernmental delegation, that could increase flexibility.

Regarding the West and the principle of the equality of provinces, we view Westerners' demand for more influence at the centre as a reasonable one. And we think that creating an effective and elected Senate would be a good way to redress the current imbalance. We support an elected, effective Senate with proportionately much more representation for the West. But we do not agree that the principle of the equality of the provinces justifies equal representation in a reformed Senate. This view stems from a misunderstanding of the basis of provincial equality. To insist on the equality of the provinces would not only put Prince Edward Island on an equal footing with Ontario, but also reduce the representation of the largely French-speaking province of Quebec – nearly a quarter of Canada's population – to a 10 percent share of senators. This would require that French-speaking Quebecers endorse a basis for representation that ignores their own distinctness.

The goal of Senate reform should be to protect the major regional, linguistic and cultural forms of diversity in the federation. While the House of Commons is based on the liberal principle of the equality of citizens, the Senate should be based on the federalist principle of respect for diversity.

Reform of the Senate and the entrenchment of concurrent powers would require constitutional amendment. As a concluding remark, we can only reiterate that this seems unlikely in the immediate future. Nevertheless, precisely because we think that there are legitimate concerns, we expect that pressures from the West and from Quebec for changes will continue and that, sooner or later, the constitutional question will be forced back on the table.

All the same, as we have argued, much can be done short of constitutional reform. Administrative agreements, the coordination of objectives in interdependent policy areas and the elucidation of a meta-vision for Canadians are key elements of a renewal of federalism – one that could be launched sooner rather than later.

Notes

1. Government of Newfoundland and Labrador, "Constitutional Proposal: An Alternative to the Meech Lake Accord," First Ministers Conference, Ottawa, November 9-10, 1989.

2. Newfoundland Throne Speech, p. 13.

3. A Triple-E Senate is one with equal representation from each province; which has effective decision-making powers; and whose members are elected.

4. Wells, "Constitutional Proposal," pp. 3-4.

5. Clyde Wells, letter to the Right Honourable Brian Mulroney, appended to the proposals of the Government of Newfoundland and Labrador for the revision of the Meech Lake Accord, November 6, 1989.

6. Ontario, Quebec and the West each have 24 seats, and the Atlantic region has a total of 30 seats. When Newfoundland entered Confederation in 1949, it was allotted six seats.

7. See chapter 8 of this volume.

8. See, for example, Philip Resnick, "Toward a Multinational Federalism: Asymmetrical and Confederal Alternatives," in F. Leslie Seidle (ed.), *Seeking a New Canadian Partnership: Asymmetrical and Confederal Options* (Montreal: Institute for Research on Public Policy, 1994), pp. 78-84; and Kenneth McRoberts, *English Canada and Quebec: Avoiding the Issue* (Toronto: York University Press, 1991), pp. 44-53.

9. See David Milne, "Exposed to the Glare: Constitutional Camouflage and the Fate of Canada's Federation," in Seidle (ed.), *Seeking a New Canadian Partnership*, pp. 111-14.

10. Peter M. Leslie, "Asymmetry: Rejected, Conceded, Imposed," in Seidle (ed.), *Seeking a New Canadian Partnership*, p. 59.

11. Philip Resnick, Minutes of the Proceedings and Evidence of the Special Joint Parliamentary Committee on a Renewed Canada, Ottawa, December 3, 1991, p. 22:7.

12. Resnick, "Toward a Multinational Federalism," pp. 80-83.

13. *Report of the Special Joint Committee on a Renewed Canada* (Ottawa: Supply and Services Canada, 1992), p. 62.

14. It should be noted that the provinces also have a spending power and that, like the federal government, they have used it in ways that promote interdependence – for example, to develop a wide variety of support programs for the export of goods and services, as well as for provincial television networks such TV Ontario and *Radio-Québec*.

15. Quoting Daniel Elazar, Maurice Croisat writes: "Both a structure and a process, contemporary federalism expresses itself by a 'negotiated cooperation' on common problems and programs which 'rests on a commitment by all parties to enter negotiations...that aim at consensus or, barring that, an accommodation which preserves the fundamental integrity of all the partners.'" *Le fédéralisme dans les démocraties contemporaines* (Paris: Montchrestien 1992), p. 127 (author's translation).

16. Government of Canada, *Shaping Canada's Future Together: Proposals* (Ottawa: Minister of Supply and Services, September 1991), pp. 41-42.

17. At a recent meeting in Toronto provincial premiers agreed to create a new formal structure for interprovincial cooperation on a number of "national" issues. We take this as an encouraging sign. See "Premiers forge new alliance," *The Globe and Mail*, September 1, 1994, p. A1.

18. Interestingly, Resnick himself raises the question of "grey areas," but then fails to explore the implications. Presumably he regards these as more of a wrinkle than a rent in the approach. We are less optimistic; see Resnick, "Toward a Multinational Federalism," p. 81.

19. These reservations are supported by a poll reported in *The Globe and Mail* (May 20, 1994, pp. 1-2) for which Quebecers were questioned about their views on the roles of the two orders of government. While they clearly favoured a shift in power toward the province, in most areas the majority preferred concurrency over exclusive provincial jurisdiction. Stéphane Dion draws a similar conclusion in "Le fédéralisme fortement asymétrique : improbable et indésirable," in Seidle (ed.), *Seeking a New Canadian Partnership*, pp. 143-44.

10

CANADA IN A POST-INDUSTRIAL WORLD: THE CASE FOR FEDERAL PLURALISM

Federal Pluralism and Community Building

In this concluding chapter we draw together some of the main ideas developed in previous pages in order to sketch a new approach to nation building, or, perhaps preferably, "community building." In contrast to old-style nation building, we have argued that fostering national unity need rely neither on economic nationalism nor the creation of a pan-Canadian identity. In the age of global integration, the former is simply unrealistic. As for the latter, it only pits one form of nationalism against another.[1]

However, it is not enough to say, as liberals traditionally have, that the solidarity that binds together the citizens of a state is a result of their mutual respect, borne of their shared commitment to a politics based on universal principles of freedom, equality and justice. If that is the main justification for Canada's existence, it is a disturbingly weak one. And it becomes difficult to see why Canadians should continue to resist the pull of integration with the United States. There is, after all, nothing distinctively *Canadian* about equality, freedom and justice.

We maintain that, between the overly intellectual conception of community defended by liberals and the essentially cultural one behind the traditional idea of a national identity, there is middle ground. It lies in fostering a common commitment to what we call a *meta-vision*.

The meta-vision consists of an over-arching set of principles and objectives that provide the rationale for Canada. It includes a recognition of the federalist commitment to respect the regional, cultural and linguistic diversity of the country, along with an analysis indicating how these are to be weighed against liberal rights and values, when the two conflict. In a nutshell, a meta-vision must do justice to the liberal aim of founding politics on universal principles, without ignoring Canadians' unique and shared history.

Thus in chapter five we agreed with the nationalists that political community requires more than just a commitment to liberal freedom and equality, despite what liberals often argue. Nevertheless, as we said, we remain liberals. For, unlike nationalists, we deny that community requires a pre-existing national identity, or an identity the state seeks to create. The alternative is to revise the idea of liberal pluralism to include a place for community as well as individual rights.

This amounts to returning to the pluralist concept that pervaded Canadian politics before 1867 and that was essential, if not clearly stated, in achieving Confederation. According to this concept, one accepts that countries such as Canada are and should remain sociologically diverse; as a result, individual citizens often have multiple allegiances. In such a state, community building will still be aimed at promoting political cohesion, integration and stability. But this will be done by acting within the framework of an over-arching meta-vision, not by developing an over-arching national identity. Such a community-building program would be derived from four sources:

- a shared commitment to liberal principles;
- respect for Canadians' shared history, including those particular values, objectives and purposes that led to the founding of the country;
- respect for the particular forms of sociological diversity that run through Canadian history, with specific consideration for the Aboriginal "diversity" that was largely disregarded in 1867; and
- a vision for the future – that is, an agenda that promotes the over-arching values and objectives toward which the community as a whole is working.

In the approach that flows from our meta-vision, federal and provincial governments may sometimes have a special obligation to promote the interests associated with a particular cultural, linguistic or regional identity. However, the proposed plu-ralism – what we have called *federal pluralism* – would assume that no single identity embraces the whole range of a citizen's interests, the way national identities tradi-tionally have been thought to do. To say that one is a Dene or *Québécois* would thus be a way of identifying important interests that an individual has; but the same person will have other interests – economic, social and cultural – that are relatively uncon-nected to his or her membership in one of these "national" communities. Federal pluralism is essentially a response to the fact that identities are complex. And, indeed, this complexity is likely to increase.

As a result of globalization, multiple allegiances are no longer limited to the forms of diversity *within* the federation. Citizens are developing new associations, attach-ments, commitments and loyalties *beyond* Canada's borders. New "transnational" allegiances are forming based on, for example, membership in human rights organi-zations or the environmental movement. Already, this is creating tensions between different levels of interest, such as the conflict between the Canadian forestry industry and the international environmental movement.

As globalization progresses, it will further fragment citizens' allegiances. In turn, this may diminish the importance of national identities. This does not mean that the identities of, say, *Québécois*, First Nations or "English-speaking Canadians" will cease to exist or to play an important role in politics and private life. It means only that individual members of those "national" communities are becoming aware that they have politically relevant interests that, increasingly, they associate with neither a particular state nor "nation." This will make the old ideal of the nation-state – that is, a self-contained, territorially defined entity whose citizens are united by a single, over-arching identity – look increasingly anachronistic.

In analyzing the "glue" that holds Canada together, we have thus argued for a distinction between a "thick" sense of political community based on federal pluralism and the traditional idea of a national identity. We contrasted the term "political community" with the term "nation-state" to indicate two different approaches to governance and to nation building. One approach – that of nationalism and of (tradi-tional) liberalism – aims at achieving political integration and stability through a single, over-arching identity. The other – federal pluralism – aims at achieving political integration and stability through a common commitment to a meta-vision.

In our view, the political community that is Canada is by policy and implication, and to some degree by law and constitution, committed to the following over-arching principles:

- the principle of mutual interest;
- the principle of mutual aid; and
- the principles of tolerance and mutual respect.

These principles underwrite our commitment as a community to three over-arching objectives:

- the pursuit of mutual benefit through the economic union;
- the commitment to mutual support through the sharing community; and
- the promotion of tolerance and mutual respect through individual freedom and equality and through recognition of community diversity.

Each objective is linked to a key domain in which Canadians have well-defined common interests. Each principle allows us to identify the fundamental rationale by which policies that promote these common interests can be targeted to achieving one of the objectives. Together, the principles and objectives form a meta-vision. That is, they provide a general framework for defining the "national interest": insofar as individual policy initiatives can reasonably be said to promote these objectives, they are in the national interest and hence justified. The meta-vision thus provides a bridge between actual policy initiatives and a (relatively) well-defined over-arching conception of the national interest.

Mutual Interest

Canadians have a common desire to maintain the integrity of their shared economic space – that is, to ensure the free movement of goods, services, capital and labour. This is an advantage *all* parts of the country benefit from, recognize as a common asset and want to maintain. Jacques Parizeau and Lucien Bouchard also want to preserve the economic union. In a nutshell, the rational basis for the economic union is that it creates opportunities and promotes individual security. It exists because it is in the *mutual interest* of all Canadians. As long as the "cost" of maintaining it does not outweigh its benefits, there is no obvious reason why they should want to fragment their shared economic space.

Mutual Aid

Peter Leslie has recently argued for the importance of recognizing a "conceptual counterpart" to the idea of the economic union in Canadian federalism.[2] He calls this counterpart the *sharing community.* Given the great differences in the capacity of provinces to raise revenues, he contends, the commitment to the sharing community is crucial to ensure that smaller provinces are able to provide services at levels reasonably comparable to those in larger provinces. The system of transfers that has evolved around the idea of the sharing community fills a gap in the original structure of Canadian federalism and, as a result, has become an essential part of what binds the federation together.

Suppose we ask: What is the basis for the sharing community? Why, in other words, should "have" provinces share with the "have-nots?" There are at least two different kinds of responses one usually gets to this question. One answer is to say that the commitment to share is a way of "pooling and sharing risks." This argument was made in the Economic Council's 28th Annual Review. According to the Review, in Canada "the pooling and sharing of the risks generated by economic upheaval is accomplished through insurance programs to support the elderly, the unemployed, farmers, depositors, and so on. Sharing risks among regions is effected through interregional transfers...Those are vital elements of the Canadian economic union..."[3]

As the Review obliquely suggests, insofar as the basis for the sharing community is a matter of pooling and sharing risks, it rests upon the same rational foundation as the economic union, namely, the principle of mutual interest. "Pooling risks" is a way of protecting oneself. One agrees to such arrangements out of self-interest. Surely this explains, in part, the way Canadians view the sharing community. However, as it stands, it cannot be a full account. If it were, there would be far greater pressure within "have" provinces to opt out of this "insurance system." For, by and large, they do not benefit from it: they are net contributors. In short, if we are to explain the continued willingness of "have" provinces to participate in the sharing community, there must be something more than just rational self-interest behind their support.

This brings us to the second answer one hears to the question "Why should 'have' provinces share?" – namely, that Canadians continue to feel a sense of co-responsibility. In fact, the Economic Council Annual Review goes on to make just such a point. It notes that the "complex web of insurance and stabilization programs

151

in Canada reflects a strong preoccupation with equity, although in many cases the programs are also justified on efficiency grounds."[4]

We would say that the "sharing community" reflects Canadians' commitment to *mutual aid*. It is basic to our account of Canada as a political community because it is linked to the economic union in such a way that, even under conditions of transnational economic integration, it maps out a distinctively Canadian space where the economic and the social forces come together in a mutually reinforcing way. As such, it acts as a counterbalance to the destabilizing forces of transnational economic integration.

Mutual Respect

Polls suggest Canadians identify very strongly with the Charter of Rights and Freedoms and regard it as an important symbol of common identity and unity. This seems to be the case even in Quebec. But, to understand the Charter's role in Canada as a political community, we need to draw a distinction between the Charter as a *liberal* and a *federal* document.

Insofar as the Charter entrenches traditional liberal individual rights, Canada is no different from any other liberal-democratic state, such as the United States, France, Germany or Britain. Liberal rights identify and protect what is universal in individuals. Liberal rights are to be understood as a fundamental *background condition* against which any modern conception of justice and politics should be defined. Canadians' commitment to respect liberal rights does not distinguish them from any of these other countries. The distinguishing feature is the way those rights interact with, limit, and are limited by, Canada's own history.

This history is already recognized in many ways in the Charter, including through the provisions on language rights, Aboriginal rights and multiculturalism. The Charter also includes a "reasonable limits" and an "override" clause. In short, it is not only a complex document, but one that contains deep internal tensions. The values and principles it expresses reflect far more than a commitment to liberal democracy as a political philosophy. They also reflect Canadians' unique historical experience as a community: the needs, aspirations and mutual commitments of its citizens. From the point of view of Canada as a political community, the Charter thus reflects the spirit of federal pluralism. It is based on a respect for citizens and to some degree for communities.

Nevertheless, Canadians' rights discourse remains mired in a view of rights that assumes a relatively unambiguous line can be drawn between the individual and the community. In our view, rights are a means of protecting interests that are held to be especially important. Different kinds of interests merit such protection. Some can be fairly dissociated from an individual's membership in a community; others less so; and still others not at all. Each polity must strive to develop its own *vision* of liberalism. Each will have its own views about exactly how liberal rights interact with and limit one another; and each will have its own unique interests that must be balanced against the commitment to respect individual freedom.

As a liberal document, the role of the Charter in Canadian society is to protect individual freedom and equality. As a federal document, it must find room for the principal interests of subnational communities that have a special historical claim in Canada – in particular, for the interests of First Nations and Quebec. If it is to be an instrument of integration and political cohesion, there must be a balance between the federalist commitment to respect social and cultural diversity and the liberal commitment to respect the individual. We can describe the rationale behind the commitment to strive toward a balance between these two as a commitment to *mutual respect*.

Reclaiming the Middle Ground

By all accepted standards of measurement, Canada is one of the world's most successful countries. International organizations repeatedly have judged it to be the best – or in the top half dozen – out of the 180 or so countries. Our standard of living is among the highest in the world, and the distribution of wealth and opportunity among citizens one of the fairest. While our social security and income support systems need reform, they remain comparable to those anywhere. Canadians are world leaders in a number of sunrise industries, including telecommunications, aerospace, computer software and pharmaceuticals. Our universities, colleges and schools, accessible to all, offer the skills and training needed to maintain Canadians' high standard of living as we integrate into the global economy. We have "peace, order and good government" to a degree not exceeded in many, if any, other countries. We are a country of many peoples and many cultures, changing rapidly in recent years, with respect for differences and confident in our demonstrated capacity to accommodate all in peace and justice.

This book was written in the conviction that the federal system, with its basic acceptance of diversity and its capacity to adapt and change, has been essential to the success of Canada as a country, and that reclaiming these two virtues – respect for diversity and flexibility – is vital for its future.

In 1867 the Fathers of Confederation assigned to the provinces those legislative powers viewed as necessary to address the specific forms of "difference" most cherished in the regions that became Canada. All received the same powers. But in no other respect was equality identified as a feature of provincehood. Quebec was clearly recognized as "different" under the British North America Act, with unique provisions for language, property and civil rights, and Senate appointments. Special financial provisions applied to Nova Scotia and New Brunswick. Each of the next three provinces to join Confederation – Manitoba in 1870, British Columbia in 1871 and Prince Edward Island in 1873 – was granted its own special provisions, tailored to its particular economic, social or geographical circumstances.

When Alberta and Saskatchewan became provinces in 1905, the most notable difference was that they did not, as did the other provinces, acquire control of their Crown lands and natural resources, a grievance that was remedied only in 1930. The terms of Union with Newfoundland when it became a province in 1949 were more "special" and detailed than any others, covering denominational schools, transportation, economic development and detailed financial arrangements. In short, historically, the establishment of the provinces has not been based on "equality"; nor has "identical treatment" ever been the case. Indeed, the reverse is true: recognition of the provinces' differences and accommodation of them in appropriate, specific ways have been essential to the country's success.

The idea that equality of the provinces (except in legislative powers) is a feature of our federation thus has no foundation; and the claim that it is a "principle of federalism" is without ground. There is, in our federation, a principle of *regional* equality for one specific purpose. The Constitution Act, 1867 identified this as the basis of representation in the Senate. There were three regions in 1867 and four in 1915, each with the same number of Senators. That is one source of Westerners' grievances over the Senate: many feel that regional equality is a principle the federation has long outgrown. Hence the shift in emphasis to *provincial* equality.

The difficulty with Senate reform is to reach agreement on a new basis for representation for the West without leaping to the conclusion that to move away from regional equality we must embrace provincial equality. However, over the last 30 years, Canadians have fallen into an increasingly rigid manner of thinking and talking about the nature of Canada and the federal system. The Senate cannot be changed without "equality of the provinces," which is unacceptable to Quebec. Quebec cannot be accommodated without its own division of powers, which is unacceptable in the West. And extreme interpretations of the inherent right threaten to make Aboriginal self-government a tangle of agreements without underlying principles that define their relationship to the Canadian state. This has made it impossible to find a basis on which to construct workable arrangements that will address the legitimate concerns of the West, Quebec and Aboriginal peoples.

In response, we emphasize, first and foremost, the need for Canadians to reform the way they think and talk about Canada – that is, to reform their "political culture." By changing the way they think and talk about federalism, we believe they can change the way they practice it. The key lies in their capacity to adopt a meta-vision for Canadian federalism.

Beyond this, we have argued that, if the longstanding grievances in the West, Quebec and among Aboriginal peoples are to be adequately addressed, a number of practical reforms to federalism will be needed. Some require constitutional change; many do not. Some can be implemented now; others will have to wait for a more propitious moment. In concluding, it may be useful to draw together the main reforms that have been advanced in this book.

We do not argue for a new division of constitutional powers for Quebec. We do argue for clear, constitutional recognition of its undoubtedly distinct society, for an interpretation of section 1 of the Charter that makes it sensitive to Quebec's special linguistic and cultural interests and for a willingness to adopt constitutional provisions, such as concurrent powers and intergovernmental delegation, that could increase flexibility. The latter measures would likely result in special federal-provincial arrangements for a number of provinces, depending on their particular interests and needs. Such arrangements are entirely consistent with federalism as we understand it.

We support an elected, effective Senate with proportionately much greater representation for the West. But we hope the West will recognize that, in light of Canada's history and the concentration of one of our official language groups in a single province, provincial equality is not appropriate.

To insist on the equality of the provinces would not only put Prince Edward Island on an equal footing with Ontario, but also reduce the representation of the largely French-speaking province of Quebec – nearly a quarter of Canada's population – to a 10 percent share of Senators. This would require that French-speaking Quebecers endorse a basis for representation that ignores their own distinctness.

The goal of Senate reform should be to protect the major regional, linguistic and cultural forms of diversity in the federation. While the House of Commons is based on the liberal principle of the equality of citizens, the Senate should be based on the federalist principle of respect for diversity.

We believe the Charter should be applied to self-governing Aboriginal communities in ways that are sensitive to First Nations' different cultural history. We support present efforts to arrive at nonconstitutional arrangements with Aboriginal peoples that will give them local control over the design and administration of programs. We believe that the adequate protection of self-government agreements will eventually require constitutional amendment.

Insofar as these initiatives require constitutional change, some of them could be considered at the Constitutional Conference of First Ministers that must be held by 1997. While we would oppose any attempt to plunge the country into yet another round of mega constitutional negotiations, our analysis leads us to conclude that, in the end, constitutional evolution will prove inescapable. Managing the process effectively will require reason, equanimity, patience and mutual respect – in a word, accommodation.

However, our analysis of federalism and of the national unity debate is intended to underline how much can be done to renew the federation, short of constitutional reform. Meaningful reform does not begin and end with the Constitution. The system is not that rigid. Administrative agreements, the coordination of objectives in interdependent policy fields and the elucidation of a meta-vision for Canadians are key elements of a renewal that can and should be launched now.

It is time that Canadians – and especially their governments – changed the way they look at federalism and began to see it more as a process than a structure. Federal and provincial governments should take a more "functionalist" approach to defining roles and responsibilities – that is, one that defines such roles and responsibilities more by reference to specific objectives than exclusive jurisdictions.

We also strongly urge governments to cooperate to address pressing issues on two other fronts. Social policy must be reformed and public spending brought under control. Both require federal-provincial cooperation. Failure to come to terms with these could have enormous consequences for Canada. These are two areas where progress cannot wait.

In a country as large and diverse as Canada, cooperation and accommodation are essential political virtues. Without them, debate becomes polarized, and the middle ground disappears. Canada is and has always been about finding the middle ground. That is how the Fathers of Confederation arrived at the choice of federalism. Among political systems, Canada's is matchless in its capacity to balance diversity with integration. Without cooperation and accommodation, however, federalism degenerates into factionalism, and diversity becomes a cacophony of competing demands.

Over the next year, as the people of Quebec approach a referendum on their future, these two virtues – cooperation and accommodation – will be especially important. Doctrinaire arguments that Canada can only be defined in this or that way will be hurled with great force, as partisans set about casting the referendum as a stark choice between separation and the *status quo*. In reply, we have argued that the choice is a spurious one. There is a third option. The middle ground is still there, if Canadians wish to reclaim it.

Notes

1. An example is found in the draft of proposed amendments to the Constitution submitted by Newfoundland Premier Clyde Wells to the First Ministers Conference in November 1989. The document was presented as an alternative to the Meech Lake Accord, in which Quebec was recognized as a distinct society.

In Premier Wells' proposal Aboriginal peoples, Canada's multicultural heritage and the existence of French- and English-speaking people were all recognized as "fundamental characteristics" of Canada. Quebec's "distinctness" was then defined by reference to one of these "fundamental characteristics" as well as by its use of the Civil Code. In marked contrast, the opening clause of Wells' proposed amendments recognized "Canada as a federal state with a distinct national identity."

It is not difficult to see why this "alternative" to the Meech Lake Accord so offended nationalists (including moderate ones) in Quebec. It implied that Quebec's "national identity" (and also that of Aboriginal peoples) has been incorporated into a larger, pan-Canadian national identity, to which it has contributed certain "fundamental characteristics." Quebec nationalists' fear that pan-Canadianism is an attempt to "folklorize" their identity thus begins to look justified in Clyde Wells' view of Canada.

See Government of Newfoundland and Labrador, "Constitutional Proposal: An Alternative to the Meech Lake Accord," First Ministers Conference, Ottawa, November 9-10, 1989.

2. Peter M. Leslie, "The Fiscal Crisis of Canadian Federalism," in *A Partnership in Trouble: Renegotiating Fiscal Federalism* (Toronto: C.D. Howe Institute, 1993), pp. 6-9.

3. Economic Council of Canada, *A Joint Venture: The Economics of Constitutional Options*, 28th Annual Review (Ottawa: Economic Council of Canada, 1991), p. 33.

4. Economic Council of Canada, *A Joint Venture*, p. 33.

NOTES ON THE AUTHORS

Donald G. Lenihan holds a doctorate in political theory. He is the former editor of *The Network/Le Réseau*, a national publication on constitutional issues, and is currently Research Associate at the Canadian Centre for Philosophy and Public Policy at the University of Ottawa.

Gordon Robertson was Clerk of the Privy Council and Secretary to the Cabinet, Government of Canada, from 1963 to 1975. From 1975 to 1979, he was Secretary to the Cabinet for Federal-Provincial Relations. During the constitutional conferences from 1968 to 1979, he served as Principal Constitutional Advisor to Prime Ministers Pearson and Trudeau.

Roger Tassé was Deputy Minister in the Department of Justice, Government of Canada, during the discussions that led to patriation of the Constitution; special advisor to the federal government during the Meech Lake Accord negotiations; senior constitutional advisor to the Special Joint Committee on a Renewed Canada (Beaudoin-Dobbie Committee); and a member of the Citizens' Forum on Canada's Future (Spicer Commission).